The Logic of Classical Liberalism
Ethics, Society, and Economics

Jacques de Guenin

Translated from the French Logique du Libéralisme
by Dennis O"Keeffe, Ph.D.

Original French Edition published by
INSTITUT CHARLES COQUELIN
Paris, France

I0104450

Expanded English Edition

For Odette

Liberty Publishing Company LLC

♦*LPC*

The Logic of Classical Liberalism: Ethics, Society, and Economics

Translated from the French edition by Dennis O'Keeffe, Ph.D.
First English Edition published July 4, 2011

Cover and design by Sitebiz (www.sitebiz.com) and set in Minion Pro and Bell Gothic Std types.

Printed and bound in the United States of America and elsewhere

The Logic of Classical Liberalism: Ethics, Society, and Economics
-by de Guenin, Jacques
-1st ed.
-p. cm

ISBN-13: 978-0-9749694-7-3 (paperback: alk. paper)
ISBN-10: 0-9749694-7-8

1. Title [1. Political Science - Essays 2. Economics - Essays]

FIRST PRINTING

Liberty Publishing Company LLC   **LPC**
www.libertypublishingcompany.com

E-mail addresses:

General inquiries: info@libertypublishingcompany.com
Media contact: media@libertypublishingcompany.com

Words of Praise About The Logic of Classical Liberalism:

(Translation of French reviews on Logique du Libéralisme)

"The Logic of Classical Liberalism is a classic work that should appear in the book collection of every reader of these lines, side by side with the immortal Economics in One Lesson of Henry Hazlitt! Both books should appear in the basic collection of any student who wishes to understand the world in which he lives."
--Professor Guy Millière in Les 4 Vérités.
(The 4 Truths: www.les4verites. com)

"You have written the little work that should be recommended to all those needing to strengthen their (classical) liberalism or to discover it or to deepen it."
--Professor Pascal Salin, former president, the Mont Pélerin Society
(www. MontPelerin.org)

"Thanks to Jacques de Guenin for having reminded us with such a clarity the consequences of the logic of (classical) liberalism."
--Le Cri du Contribuable
(The Cry of the Taxpayer: www.lecri.fr)

The book shows that the various concepts of (classical) liberalism follow each other by an implacable logic, from moral foundations to economic life, by way of the functioning of society. But although it emphasizes the moral aspect of (classical) liberalism, it also shows that the (classical) liberal philosophy generates the most efficient societies.
--Liberté Chérie
(Beloved Freedom Association: www.liberte-cherie.com)

Jacques de Guenin expresses the idea that the only way for a government to achieve full employment is to back out entirely from the labor market, leaving employers and employees to contract freely.
--Toqueville Magazine
(www.libeco.net)

Contents

Conclusion: The Future - What is to be Done?   **111**

Appendices:

Publisher's Foreword to the US Edition

Congratulations! You hold in your hand a book destined to become one of the great classics in Liberal thought.

Words have precise meanings. However, over time, sometimes a word in one culture comes to mean the opposite of what it originally meant. And sometimes such a word will retain its original meaning in other cultures and not in ours. For example, the word "awful" originally meant "deserving of awe". Now it popularly means "terrible". A "public school" in England is quite private. In the U.S. it is run by the State - it means just the opposite thing.

In the nineteenth century, the word "liberal" meant the same thing in Europe and the United States.

A liberal was a tolerant person who believed in the values taught by the US Constitution's Bill of Rights. A liberal was a lover of freedom. First and foremost, a liberal was a person who believed that the rights of the individual come before those of the State. The liberal believed that "small was good", that the State was a necessary evil and thus it's all-reaching powers over its citizens should be limited. Checks-and-balances would be created to protect the rights of the individual against the State. Society was seen to be created from the bottom-up, made up of individuals who came together voluntarily to share their existence in a free marketplace, and whose rights were unalienable and God-given, not those arbitrarily granted by a King or dictator.

As the author, Jacques de Guerin writes, liberal morality is altruistic: it teaches respect for the liberty of others.

This was Liberalism, and it is still called that today in Europe. In the United States, it is often substituted by "libertarianism", or "classical liberalism", an awkward phrase but, unfortunately, necessary. Thus our book's U.S. title.

How did the word liberal come to mean exactly the opposite in the U.S. as what it used to mean - and still means in Europe today? How was its meaning stolen and perverted?

"Socialism, on the other hand, is concerned with the collective. It regards society as an entity whose existence is independent of the elements composing it", writes the author.

By the 1930's, the socialist, Franklin D. Roosevelt, had become the President of the United States running as a Democrat. During WWII, the National Socialists (Nazi's) in Germany and the Soviet Socialists in the USSR had tarred the name "socialism" in the American people's mind. To separate themselves from "socialists", the Democrats proceeded to appropriate the name "liberal" from the libertarians in Europe. Over time, "liberal" in the U.S. came to mean Democrat party ideals of big government, big union, big business, and big State control. By the 1990's, Americans came to see "Liberalism" as being synonymous with "Socialism-Lite" or just plain Socialism itself.

That's why this book in American English is entitled "The Logic of Classical Liberalism". In French, it's title reads simply: "The Logic of Liberalism" Apologies to Canadian and British readers who know the difference between Liberalism and Socialism and have often wondered why the newfangled word "Libertarianism" is used in the United States to describe true liberal ideals and thoughts!

Introduction

Properly speaking there are only two philosophies of man in society: Liberalism, based on the individual, and Socialism, based on the collectivity. All the others are derived, more or less, from one or the other.

In the nineteenth century, the word "Liberal" had the same meaning in Europe and in the Anglo-Saxon world. In the United States, however - and to a lesser extent in Great Britain - the meaning of the word has been intentionally redefined progressively toward the left of the political spectrum by the Socialists. Thus a precise translation of the French word (Libéral) would be "classical liberal". To avoid the repetition of the adjective "classical", we have decided, by convention, to use the word "liberal" with its original authentic nineteenth-century meaning.

Liberalism is concerned with the individual. It regards society as composed of free and responsible individuals, who interact by way of exchange, or gifts or associations. It holds that any individual action in favor of others should be carried out freely, perhaps by a reasoned process or perhaps by inclination, but never by coercion. It studies society by the method known as "methodological individualism" which proceeds from the individual to the general. Thus Liberalism explains the actions of the State in terms of the individual motivations of the people holding power, and history in terms of the impact of individuals on the evolution of societies.

Socialism, by contrast, is concerned with the collective. It regards society as an entity whose existence is independent of the elements composing it. It holds that individuals should obey rules set down by society. Its study of society aggregates data, using statistics and macroeconomic reasoning. It groups individuals into classes. Socialism regards the historical process as subject to laws operating independently of individuals.

These two philosophies are clearly incompatible. Applied by politicians to social life they yield irreducibly different results. All attempts to reconcile them by a search for "a Third Way" have served only to engender contradictions, the costs of which individuals have to pay for.

Liberals strive to understand the nature of man and to deduce from it rules of individual behavior compatible with it. This is why we find such coherence across the writings of the great liberal thinkers of history, from Lao Tse to Rothbard, by way of Aristotle, Locke, Smith, Montesquieu, Turgot, Constant, Say, Cobden, Bastiat, J.S. Mill, Toqueville, Molinari, Von Mises, Ayn Rand, and Hayek, among those who are best known in the West.1.

The great socialist authors, by contrast, do define the ideal society according to their own perspective, with the latter varying considerably from author to author, from Plato to Stalin by way of Babeuf, Owen, Saint-Simon, Fourrier, Jaurès, Gramsci, Blum, Engels, Marx, Lenin, Troksky, and Mao Ze Dong.

There are so many books of high quality on liberalism, that one can fairly ask whether the latter can bear the weight of any more. All the great authors mentioned above, however, have in the event developed this or that aspect of liberalism, and if there are today excellent syntheses by talented contemporary authors, there exists, so far as I know, no account aiming to show that the various concepts of liberalism follow, each from its predecessor, by an implacable logic, from moral foundations to economic life, by way of the functioning of society.

Such is the object of this book. The first part deals with the interconnected moral tenets of liberalism - individual freedom, responsibility, respect for life, the quest for happiness, property - in order to bring out this mutual interdependence. The second part is devoted to the kind of society which derives from the respect for these moral principles. The third deals with the economic consequences of the first and second parts, consequences which include the free market and capitalism.

I am deeply grateful to Judith Lazar, Pierrette Morin and to my wife Odette, for their encouragement, as well as for their detailed and remorseless scrutinizing of my text, along with their suggestions. I also wish to acknowledge the assistance of my translator, Professor Dennis O'Keeffe, an able scholar in political economy, and my U.S. publisher and editor Terry Easton, for having helped me to adapt for the English and the American readers, respectively, the parts that were excessively specific to the French context.

Jacques de Guenin
Saint Loubouer, France
Spring 2011

Part One:

The Moral Foundations of Liberalism

Chapter 1. Individual Freedom

No man has the right to initiate the use of physical force against others.
Ayn Rand

Liberalism is based entirely upon the idea of individual freedom. All the other concepts commonly attached to liberalism, such as responsibility, the respect for life, and property, follow from it by a rigorous logic, as this book aims to demonstrate. It is therefore imperative to begin by defining clearly what individual freedom is, all the more so because its grounds are frequently misrepresented in a way damaging to liberalism, which saddles it with an unfounded hostility.

The liberal does not look for his own dear liberty at the expense of others. Wanting everyone to be free, he seeks the freedom of the next fellow. Article 4 of the French Declaration of the Rights of Man and the Citizen in 1789 has the best formulation:

Freedom consists in being able to do everything which does not harm other people; thus the exercise of natural rights has no limits other than those which assure to other members of society the enjoyment of these same rights.

Contrary to the charge often laid against liberalism, liberal morality is altruistic: it teaches respect for the liberty of others. As for a famous French sophism: "liberalism is the free fox in the free henhouse he is free to enter", it serves only to identify the ignorance of those who pronounce it. In truth the liberal is on the side of the chickens and is often devoured by the fox as he seeks to protect them. This point is worth driving home. Liberalism is not for the strong to have the freedom to do what they like to the detriment of the weak. Liberalism is the protection of the weak against the exactions of the strong. To wish an individual to be free is to forbid oneself to obtain anything from him by coercion, above all by violent means. The liberal has therefore renounced violence. If he wants to bring someone round to his ideas, he uses only example or discussion. If he wishes to obtain from another any good or benefit of any kind, he will proceed only by way of a freely agreed voluntary exchange.

The contours of individual freedom are not always entirely clear. Thus many people who believe themselves to be liberal think that everyone must be free to make such use of alcohol and drugs as he sees fit. It is for him only to evaluate consequences and to make his choice. However, things are not that simple, since one's consequences can affect other people. A person might kill someone if he drives when he is drunk, beats his wife if he comes to grief with alcoholism, or becomes a financial burden on society if he makes excessive use of drugs.

This is a subject we will come back to in relation to responsibility. Let us simply note at this stage that authentic liberalism calls us to be virtuous. But how is this to be achieved?

The feeling that every individual must be left free to act and pursue his destiny as he will, is not, it seems, innate in mankind. The world is full of people who seek only to subject others to their control. It is also true, however, that many people accommodate themselves well, even voluntarily, to a certain dependency upon others. A guardian state, or even an enlightened dictatorship, are considered by many to be acceptable, comfortable even, or even desirable. Thus the liberal order is not a spontaneous order, and many people even ask whether it is not a utopian one. It is apparent that the road we must follow to get to it is beset with snares. For example, we often think of the State when we want to have our individual freedom protected, though the State has always been the main source of coercion.

Liberals think we have to surmount these obstacles for three sets of reasons.

First, for some, each individual has an inalienable right to his freedom, and we all have a morally binding duty to respect this right, without regard to any other consideration. Amongst the most radical defenders of this view are Ayn Rand and Murray Rothbard.

Second, for the vast majority of liberals, freedom is desirable on the grounds of its positive consequences. Everywhere it is respected, it permits each person to fulfill himself, it favors the enlargement, the flowering, of the individual, and is a source of general prosperity. Liberals of this stripe are sometimes defined as 'utilitarian'.

Third, liberalism is logically coherent. None of the other doctrines claiming to seek the good of humankind can pass the test of non-contradiction. They subsist only because nobody takes the trouble to submit them to rigorous exegesis, that is, to the test of logical truth. Ideas always have consequences.

The trouble is that a society which is based on contradictory ideas, cannot help but throw up dysfunctions in the social order.   Utopias always deteriorate into Dystopias, and millions of people suffer death and deprivation because of illogical, faulty and corrupting ideas.

This book would not be very useful, however, if we were content to demonstrate that the liberal social order is the best possible or logical one for the individual or society as a whole. We still need to raise the issue as to the means of achieving this order.

Some "means" may be "good", and "moral". Other means may be "evil" and "immoral". In exploring these issues, we will seek to show that liberalism is deeply moral, and its anthesis, socialism, is profoundly immoral.

Some pages will be devoted to this question.

Chapter 2. Responsibility

Responsibility is the essence of the free man's self-respect
Alain Laurent[1]

It ought not to be necessary to add the adjective "individual" to the word "responsibility", since the concept of "collective responsibility" is meaningless. Sad to say, however, this latter idea became fashionable during the course of the twentieth century, when a quite specifically collectivist philosophy bit by bit made its way into schools, universities, governments, political parties and the State itself in various European countries - as well as the United States itself.. This socialist philosophy claims that human beings do not really enjoy free will and are therefore not fully responsible for their acts. It reaches its extreme with the sociologist Bourdieu, for whom the idea of individual responsibility is petit-bourgeois (or "middle class"), this being the epithet to which Marxists resort when they are forced to replace arguments whose inconsistency can no longer be disguised, with emotive appeals.

One does not have to look very far into the works of these authors to see that they fail the test of non-contradiction. Thus, according to their way of thinking, if an employee makes a blunder, it must be his employer who is responsible. Big Brother and the Nanny State grow naturally out of this belief in the irresponsibility of the individual and the organizations he voluntarily creates with other individuals.

The philosopher Saint-Exupéry stated the (in)famous maxim "each person has sole responsibility for all (others)"[2] Saint-Exupéry was a great writer, the author of many novels, vibrant with human feeling and featuring strong and compelling heroes. But why in heaven's name did he surrender himself to punctuating his work with foolish sophisms of this kind? The

---

1 This quote is taken from a lecture given by Alain Laurent to the Frédéric Bastiat Circle in March 1999. The whole text can be found on the website www.bastiat.net, in the section "les activités du Cercle Frédéric Bastiat", "les textes des précédents diners-débats". Several of the ideas found in this chapter come from this lecture.
2 *Night Flight*, 1931 (French title: Vol de Nuit)

phrase "each person has sole responsibility for all (others)" sounds pretty enough, but it is meaningless. If you doubt this, try to give it a meaning. At the very most it serves to make weak minds feel guilty. Sad to say, it has had progeny.

Today, if one is to believe the collectivists of all stripes, it is worthy souls like the liberals who are responsible for all the suburban violence. In France, the socialist Françoise Giroud, has written in the national L'Express newspaper "we are all responsible for the young delinquents" The executioner has become the victim, whilst the victim is abandoned to his sad lot. Indeed he is lucky if he is not he who suffers the punishment of the law.

A similar statement was made by Hillary Clinton years ago when she repeated the African bush statement "it takes a village to raise a child". This implies collective rather than "only" individual responsibility.

Back in France, the socialist politician Martine Aubry considered the possibility of holding the doctors in a given area "collectively responsible" if some of them saw more patients then the rules allowed! This drift in thinking towards injustice, fuzziness and inconsistency has played no small part in the slide of free countries towards mediocrity - and collapse. "When words lose their sense, people lose their liberty" as the Chinese philosopher Lao Tse said two and a half thousand years ago.

As we did with the concept of freedom, let us now give a precise definition of "responsibility", in order to be able to build on it irrefutable arguments. "To be responsible means to take on the consequences of one's own actions". Therefore there cannot be so-called collective responsibility.

The concepts of freedom and responsibility are dependent upon each other. One cannot exist without the other. In fact one cannot be responsible for one's acts unless one is free to commit them - or not. The concept of responsibility therefore clearly entails that of freedom. The reciprocal is also clear: the idea of freedom entails responsibility. If one wishes to respect the freedom of others, one must take on one's own shoulders the consequences of one's own actions. One must not impose on others the burden of one's own errors or imprudence.

In his Nichomachean Ethics, the ancient Greek philosopher

Aristotle says that man must account for his actions once he has taken the initiative for them. He asserts that man is actually responsible for his irresponsibility. If a drunken man causes an accident or commits a murder, many people say he is not responsible because he doesn't know what he is doing. Aristotle denies this. For him, perhaps the drunken man doesn't know what he is doing at the moment of the accident but he is responsible when he takes the decision to drink. Whatever he may do, a man always decides for himself.

Liberals, who regard the respect for the freedom of others as morally imperative, therefore necessarily regard responsibility as a correlative obligation which is absolute. Utilitarian liberals see this as having practical advantages too.

First of all this is a principle of step by step learning and self-improvement.

"Responsibility", Frédéric Bastiat tells us, "is the natural linkage which exists, in respect of the active being, between the act and its consequences(....). Its purpose is obviously to restrict the number of bad actions, to enlarge the number of good ones...

From earliest childhood to extreme old age, our life is nothing but one long apprenticeship. We learn to walk by falling; we learn by harsh and repeated experiences to avoid heat, cold, hunger, thirst and various excesses. Let us not complain that the experiences are harsh; if they were not, we would not learn anything." (Economic Harmonies)

True, errors due to inexperience are pardonable. The responsible man, however, assumes the authorship of his acts and strives not to repeat his mistakes. The opposite course would be for him to deny his negligence, claim ignorance, and scorn the people who have accused him.

Responsibility is also a source of self fulfillment. There is no shortage of people who agree to take on responsibilities or even search them out. To exercise one's responsibility is also to experience the joy of employing one's strength, one's spirit of enterprise, one's initiative, and the pride of proving one's worth. We often see little advertisements to the effect that "we are looking for somebody to be "responsible for sales", or "responsible for accounting". Does one imagine for an instant that one would find candidates if a certain pride was not associated with the words "responsible"? An adolescent - even a child - aspires to be responsible for himself. When a child is trusted to act responsibly, he is proud of it, he wants to show that he is capable of doing what is asked of him, and he does everything he can to this end. So we should not see responsibility only in negative terms of the punishment of error, but also in positive terms of the potential that each human being has to fulfill himself.

Chapter 3. Respect for Life, Effort, Reason and the Search for Happiness

We receive from God the gift which subsumes them all, Life, - physical, intellectual and moral life. But life is not self-sustaining on its own. He who gave it to us has given us the burden of sustaining it, developing it, perfecting it. To this end He has given us a marvelous set of faculties. He has plunged us into a milieu of diverse elements. It is through the application of these faculties that the phenomenon of assimilation, of appropriation is realized, by which life completes the circle which has been assigned to it."

Frédéric Bastiat[1]

All the functions of all living beings, from the simplest to the most complex, have the maintenance of their life as their first objective. Each living being must procure for itself the energy or the food which it needs to live, to propagate and to protect itself from external threats. It must react to external conditions or to aggression by its actions. In the case of plants or lower animals, these actions are entirely automatic and unconscious. Man, however, is characterized by his awareness of exterior conditions. They register themselves through pain and pleasure.

To the objective of preserving his life, man adds the further purpose of maximizing his satisfactions, or in other language, of seeking happiness. To support his life and to seek for happiness he possesses marvelous faculties, including a brain sufficiently developed for him to conceive objectives and to direct his actions to attaining them. The price of these actions is effort. Their result will be to increase or diminish his satisfaction. His brain also enables him to memorize the outcomes of these actions, to analyze them, and to draw conclusions as to how to improve on them. What is involved here is that critical faculty we call "reason".

It is apparent that through efforts and the use of his reason, man can progress indefinitely in his search for happiness, subject to two conditions:

- That he is free in his actions.
- That he assumes responsibility for their consequences.

---

1   The Law, 1850 (French title: La Loi)

If he possesses freedom, man can create new possibilities. If he takes responsibility for their consequences, he can take advantage of his mistakes to his further benefit.

Thus we take up again now the two basic principles we recounted in earlier chapters: freedom and responsibility.

A man will get better results in proportion to his efforts and his reason. He will do better than the idle and those who act without thinking. Herein lies a useful source of inequality, for he who succeeds by way of working and thinking furnishes an example to others. By contrast is it not profoundly unjust to reward in the same way both the idle fellow and the one who takes care and effort in what he does? Or he who acts carelessly and he who thinks carefully? Liberalism is not about equality of outcomes. In this it marks itself off from socialism. Liberalism is not about the equality of "ends". It is about the just and proper use of "means" Thus, to the liberal, the famous quote of Niccolo Machiavelli: "the ends justify the means", beloved by Marx, is false, if not dangerous.

On the other hand liberalism rejects as immoral inequalities based on coercion: slavery, legal inequalities, the caste system, privileges granted to such and such a category of citizens, notably to those who hold power, under the pretext that they constitute an elite avant-garde for the masses of the population.

It is good to recall that at the outbreak of the French Revolution, it was the liberals, in particular Lafayette, who brought about the abolition of the elites' privileges. Lafayette, of course, fought side-by-side with George Washington to support the liberal American cause of freedom against a tyrannical king.

More important still, liberals were the avant-garde in the struggle against slavery. A movement of opinion, launched by a "society of friends of the blacks" was energized by liberals like Diderot, Condorcet, Lafayette, and the Abbé Grégoire. The Abbé strove to have the Convention adopt a Decree of Abolition, which after long struggles he managed to obtain on February 4th 1794. Sadly, Bonaparte reestablished slavery under the Consulate, on May 20th 1802. The fight for abolition restarted under the Second Republic, inspired essentially by liberals, including Frédéric Bastiat, Victor Hugo, Tocqueville, Montalembert, and above all Victor Schoelcher, who succeeded in getting slavery abolished definitively on April 27th 1848.

By the 1860's, similar moral liberal battles were also taking place, culminating with Abraham Lincoln's abolition of slavery during the Civil War.

In the previous chapter we showed first that the concept of responsibility is derived logically from that of individual freedom,. Then we examined all the supplementary resources it affords the individual. In the same way, after we have shown that the search for happiness cannot be separated from individual freedom and responsibility, we will go on to demonstrate the full richness of this concept.

Liberalism is a hymn to life, effort, reason, and the search for happiness. Liberal philosophers who have written novels, such as Diderot, Voltaire, Victor Hugo and Ayn Rand, feature heroes who are positive, thoughtful, enterprising, who surmount obstacles in their way and seek to fulfill themselves.

The most distinguished American liberal philosophical magazine is called Reason. It is a review of modern "classical liberal" - or libertarian - principles and issues.

The Second Paragraph of the Declaration of American Independence, adopted by Congress on the fourth of July 1776 (Independence Day) begins as follows: "We hold these truths to be self-evident, that all men are created equal, that they are endowed by their creator with certain inalienable Rights, that among these are Life, Liberty and the pursuit of Happiness. This text was drafted by Thomas Jefferson and revised by Benjamin Franklin and John Adams, men of fundamentally liberal outlook.

Ayn Rand emphasized the precise wording of the text. It does not say that men have a right to happiness. It says that they have a right to look for it. This means that men have the right, that is to say the freedom, to undertake courses of action, for which they assume the responsibility, in order to increase their satisfactions. This does not mean that any other party, including the State, must procure these for them. These are the distinctions we will return to in the chapters on the Rights of Man and The State.

The importance accorded by liberals to life and the pursuit of happiness is entirely at one with their rejection of all coercion. Obviously, Communism, on the contrary, is marked by the short shrift it gives to individuals when it is in power. As for socialism, while it is certainly true that in its modest versions it does not menace people's lives, it does systematically encourage a feeling of guilt among those who succeed, even when that success is the fruit of their efforts and of the application of their reason. Thus they can the more easily confiscate a part of that fruit and redistribute it as the government wills.

Chapter 4. Property

The purpose of all political association is the conservation of the natural and imprescriptible rights of man. These rights are freedom, property, security, and resistance to oppression.
French Declaration of the Rights of Man and the Citizen, 1799, Article 2.

A quotation from Frédéric Bastiat, taken from The Law, introduced the last chapter. It began with the question of Life, the subject of that chapter, and ended with the idea of appropriation, making clear thereby, the narrow link between life and property, the subject of the present chapter. In an earlier pamphlet, Property and Law, Bastiat had already developed this theme by bringing to it several clarifications:

"I understand by property", he writes, "the right the worker has to the value of anything he has created by his labor", adding later: "I point out first of all, that I use the word property in its general sense, and not in the restricted meaning of landed property. I regret, and probably all economists share my regret, that this word evokes in us, involuntarily on our part, the idea of the ownership of the soil"

Then he writes:

"Man is born a proprietor, because he is born with needs whose satisfaction is indispensable to life, and with organs and faculties without which these needs cannot be satisfied. The faculties are nothing more than the extension of the person; property is only the extension of the faculties. To separate a man from his faculties is to condemn him to death. So is separating him from the product of his faculties".

He continues:

"Man lives and develops himself by accumulating property. Such appropriation is a natural and providential phenomenon, crucial to life, and property is only appropriation on which labor has conferred the status of a right. When work has made substances capable of constituting property which previously were not, I do not see how anyone could rightfully claim that this property formation could be effected to the advantage of any individual other than he who performed the labor.

To secure his life, man must produce goods he can consume, store or exchange, and services he can exchange for other goods and services. He who has no right to the product of his labor has no certainty of being able to manage his life in the way he wishes. The man who produces while others dispose of what he produces is a slave. Private property acquired by effort and reason, is therefore an imperative condition of the exercise of freedom.

He who produces and exchanges has earned what he possesses thanks to his efforts. He has accumulated nothing which is not merited. He does not count on being paid for his good looks or any complaining he does, or for passively registering his needs, but rather on what he produces, on what he has accomplished. The reciprocal to this is that property acquired by force, theft or deceit, is formally at odds with the liberal morality such as we have recounted it thus far.

A century and a half before Bastiat, in his Second Treatise on Civil Government (1690), John Locke had developed a theory of property which still rings authoritatively with liberals.[1] In good liberal fashion, he showed first of all that there exists a form of property whose legitimacy is incontestable: the ownership of self, a corollary of individual freedom, such as we defined it in the first chapter.[2] It follows from the notion that man is necessarily the owner of his labor, but also of the fruits of that labor, and by extension of the objects, including the soil, with which he has mingled his labor, and which hitherto belonged to no one.

For the liberal, property is essentially individual. To satisfy objectives that go beyond his individual capacities, however, the individual associates freely with other individuals, to form associations or enterprises, which we will talk about in Parts Two and Three. These voluntary membership associations, often called "corporations", "partnerships" or "legal entities"

---

1   This has not prevented this theory's being deepened and enriched, as Henri Lepage shows very well in his very informative and comprehensive book *Pourquoi la propriété* (*Why Property*, published by Hachette; Collection Pluriel, 1985). Several of the ideas that follow are taken from his book.

2   In this way he enriched the thinking which was to later result in the abolition of slavery.

have the right to own property. In that sense we can speak of property jointly owned. This does not carry the same meaning as the socialist term "collective property" which in reality means the property of the State. Although today's "socialist" countries have now dropped the notion, socialism has for long been defined as the public ownership of the means of production and exchange. Even today, however, socialism clings to the idea that the land itself belongs to the State, which is kind enough to allow individuals some use of it. Thus when the French socialists arrived in power in 1981, they did not take long to institute a new urban code which in its first article, Article L110, surreptitiously slipped in this monstrous violation of property rights, passing virtually unnoticed among the host of measures aiming at the re-collectivization of France:

"The territory of France is the common patrimony (inheritance) of the nation. Each local community is its guardian and manager within the limits of its jurisdiction".

In a lecture given in 1980 to the Mont Pèlerin Society[3], entitled 'Capitalism under the Test of Ethics', Professor Arthur Shenfield expressed himself as follows:

" Because it requires care and attention", he writes, " property is a veritable school of morality. This is the lesson we learn from him who manages his wealth as a " good father of his family" a figure so often cited by way of example in traditional works of morality (...) The moral value of property arises because it encourages its owner to treat it as one treats things of which one is no more than the trustee, in the name of children and grand-children, to whom one expects one day to leave it. To be persuaded of this, it suffices for us to observe the contrast which appears in our attitude,   once we are dealing with collective rather than private property; the negligence which we generally display once we are using public property. And the behavior one sees in the so-called socialist

---

3   The Mont Pèlerin Society was founded by Friedrich Hayek, Ludwig von Mises, Milton Friedman, and other "Austrian School" economists in 1947 to keep the spirit of liberalism going in a world increasingly menaced by collectivism. It numbers today over 500 members, including several of the living recipients of the Nobel Prize for Economics. It meets at least once a year in various parts of the planet. Today it is probably the most prestigious Economics society in the world.

societies will not make liars of us". [4]

Like the earlier features of liberalism that we have been looking at so far, while private property rests above all on moral considerations, it has proven its practical efficacy. This efficacy comes from its personal, exclusive and freely transferable quality.

Exclusive ownership of a good permits the owner to make the best possible use of it, as was very vividly shown by the collectivization of land in the USSR. On the tiny plots of land allowed to each agricultural worker, plots whose products the workers were allowed to sell freely on the local market, such marketable products - the kind consumers were looking for - carried the day over the products of the kolkhoz (collective farm). This was true even though the kolkhoz had far more power, distribution, and land., It is recognized by historians that without these private plot contributions, entire regions would have experienced famine...a point grudgingly acknowledged by the Soviet State, which otherwise would never have allowed such doctrinal infractions.

The free transferability of a good tends to direct it towards those who will make the best use of it. Individuals do not all have the same capabilities and   aptitudes, nor the same motivation for the careful management of what belongs to them. Thanks to the process of exchange, which we will be talking about in Part Two, goods are directed little by little towards those who have the ability and motivation to make the most efficient use of them, provided that free trade prevails. Since in free exchange, each person receives his due and no one is slighted, the generalizing of this process enables a growing satisfaction for everybody, and thus contributes to the well-being of each person.

Another decided advantage of property is the personal and family security which it secures in this troubled world. He who possesses nothing is not only materially deprived, but also psychologically weakened. This is why many people seek to own their own dwelling-places, even when they are satisfied with those they rent. With precisely the opposite intention, to weaken the potential resistance of the Jews, the Nazis began dispossessing them of their possessions. In the same way, in order to ensure the docility of the population, the communists - everywhere they took power - began

---

4   Quoted by Henri Lepage in *Pourquoi la propriété (Why Property)*?

by abolishing private property.

We will round off our logical progression through the moral foundations of liberalism, a progression which has occupied these first four chapters, with a quote from Murray Rothbard: "Freedom is the right to do what one wishes with one's own".[5] As Henri Lepage puts it in Why Property? this dictum contains within itself the restriction placed in the first Chapter on Individual Freedom: individual freedom begins at the boundary where the freedom of others stops. Its essence is that two individuals cannot in the very order of things have a right to the same object, since its appropriation is legitimate only for him whose efforts created it or who obtained it in free exchange.

Thus we rediscover the idea of freedom flowing from that of property. Since we derived the idea of property from that of freedom by means of a logical sequence, the cycle is now complete.

---

5   *Power and Market*, Institute for Humane Studies, Sheed, Andrews and McNeal, 1970.

Chapter 5. Links with Judeo-Christian Morality

God has made me with free will. If I have sinned, it is I who have sinned. I and not fate, chance, the Devil... None of them forced me.

Saint Augustine[1]

Liberalism having developed within Western society, it is reasonable to enquire whether its moral perspective is compatible with the Judeo-Christian morality which has permeated the West for many centuries. The answer is not evident a priori, since liberalism begins with the Enlightenment, whose rationalism was in part a rebellion against a Religion which had lost its spirit of criticism. Several of the philosophers of the century of Enlightenment (although not all) were agnostic or atheist. Today many liberals (although not all) still tend to be agnostic or atheist. Whatever the case may be, liberalism claims no credentials from any religion, nor has any religion declared in favor of liberalism, and yet there is clear compatibility between liberal morality and the Judeo-Christian morality of the Old Testament and the Christian morality of the New Testament, even if the precise wordings are not identical.

The underlying link between these different world views is the notion of free will. For Jews and Christians each individual is unique and possesses free will, given by God. We began this chapter with a quotation from Saint Augustine because he has more commonly been associated with the concepts of Divine Grace and predestination, unlike other Catholic thinkers of his era, the Pelagians, who stuck exclusively to free will. Our quotation shows that even Augustine acknowledged the fundamental importance of free will.

Sixteen centuries later, Cardinal Etchegaray, an intimate of John-Paul II, went even further in the affirmation of individual freedom: "God Himself cannot controvert the conscience of a man whom He has created free. It is conscience which has the last word, being stronger than all ideologies, all maneuvering, and even all religions".

---

1   *The Confessions,* Circa AD 400.

By contrast it is clear that collectivism cannot live comfortably alongside the Judeo-Christian religions. In fact they were pitilessly pursued in the Soviet Union. Between 1917 and 1940, 75 000 places of worship were destroyed, 600 bishops, 40 000 priests, and 12 000 monks and nuns were systematically killed. The respite granted following the Great Patriotic War did not last. Anti-religious propaganda was resumed in 1947. Khrushchev, thought of as a moderate in the West, nevertheless resumed the persecutions after 1959.

Let us move on to Judeo-Christian morality proper. Rather than getting ourselves lost meandering through the Old Testament, written by men, we will stick to the brief passage where God is said to have directly communicated to Moses the basic elements of morality in the form of the Ten Commandments. Four of these deal with the relationship between man and God. They are outside the scope of this book. The other six, however, concern the relationships of man to his fellows.

Three of the six[2] refer to the protection of life and to individual fulfillment: "honor thy father and thy mother", "thou shalt not commit adultery", "thou shalt not kill". The first requires children to take their parents' advice seriously, which will keep them clear of many dangers. The second enjoins parents to stay together, it being well known how much better children flourish in a united family than in broken homes. The third condemns violence, although less radically than liberalism, since it limits itself to specifically forbidding murder.

"Thou shalt not steal" confirms the sacred character of property. "Thou shalt not bear false witness" establishes truth-telling as one of the most fundamental virtues in the eyes of the Creator. This commandment gives the search for truth a higher status than does liberal morality, which certainly devotes much intellectual effort to the subject, but in the form of the pursuit of reason. Finally, "Thou shalt not envy what belongs to your neighbor" refocuses on the pursuit of happiness. This commandment confirms the fact that in their free and voluntary efforts

---

2   The numbering of the ten commandments and the content of each has varied according to the Bibles of the different Christian Churches, and for some of them, according to time. In this chapter, we are using the *"Ecumenical Translation of the Bible"*, published in France by a joint group of Catholic and Protestant scholars and published in 1975-1976.

to organize their lives and seek for happiness, men obtain unequal results. This commandment enjoins them to accept this and not to show any unhappiness about it. Let us remember that in the Christian religion, envy is a mortal sin, which consists in feeling distress at the good fortune of others, and rejoicing at their misfortune. Let us also note that to justify their mania for redistribution, those in power openly cultivate envy, which they camouflage with the catchword "solidarity" (or "fellowship" and "fairness").

If the vast – and vastly complex – legislation of each nation were reduced to these six commandments, it is obvious that humanity would behave much better. François Guillaumat offers this formulation: "The thief is not he who does not follow the state procedures for seizing the wealth of others, but he who seizes the wealth of another without his consent".[3] Some Christians believe in God simply because they think that the Ten Commandments are so luminous in their clarity, simplicity and efficaciousness that they cannot have been invented by men.

Did the hotchpotch created by the Prophets in the Old Testament complicate the simplicity of the divine message? Whether this be so or not, little store was set by humanity on the Ten Commandments. The Christian faith teaches that God incarnated Himself in the person of Jesus to bring things into focus. Jesus said: "I bring a new Commandment: Love one another as my father has loved you", or "You shall love your neighbor as yourself". This means that one must wish others to have, and even help them to have, that which one regards as most precious for oneself. The liberal position is identical: to obtain one's own freedom and happiness, one can never infringe upon another person's freedom and happiness.

---

3   For example in his paper *"Liberalism and Christianity"* given to the Frédéric Bastiat Circle on June 20th 1998 and available on the site www.Bastiat.net.

Part Two:

Life in Society

Chapter 6. Trade

Free trade......is breaking down the barriers that separate nations: those barriers behind which nestle the feelings of pride, revenge ,hatred and jealousy, which every now and then burst their bounds, and deluge whole countries with blood; those feelings which nourish the poison of war and conquest

Richard Cobden.[1]

Free trade (free exchange) is most commonly treated as an aspect of the economic system, and this is exactly how we will deal with it in Part Three. In the present chapter we will confine ourselves to making palpable its moral legitimacy and usefulness to society.

The relationship of the individual to his fellows much improves the effectiveness of his search, by way of reason and effort, for satisfaction in life, a subject we spoke of in Chapter 3. Comparing his success with that of others facilitates his progress, provided that he is not influenced by envy. [2]

Thus the search for efficiency leads to a positive examination of the results achieved by others, entailing the suppression of any trace of passive envy. This comparison thereby contributes to moral progress.

Reason and effort in the search for individual happiness, however, also entail extremely positive consequences for society. The free man is creative; he can devise novel approaches. He will thereby enrich others, too. The man who comes up with an idea or invention, receives only a tiny part of the value he has added to the stock of our human heritage, an addition from which countless souls will benefit.

---

1   *English Liberal Party Statesman.* From his address given at Covent Garden on 28th September 1843.

2   It is interesting to note that in Roman Catholic theology, Envy is a mortal sin, one of the Seven Cardinal Sins. It consists in being downcast at the joy of others and rejoicing in their misfortune. The convention today is to speak of "passive envy", "active envy", or emulation being on the contrary the tendency to be stimu-lated by the success of others and to try to do equally well. Socialists specialize in exploiting Envy against others who they believe "have too much".

The individual can obtain, thanks to trade, goods and services he cannot or does not wish to produce himself, the exchange being usually formalized by a contract if it ranges over a significant stretch of time. Included in this category are the buying of objects, nothing else than the exchanging of those objects for money, and earnings, which are simply the exchange of services for money. When trade is free, both of the two parties to it find it advantageous, or otherwise they would not do it. Therefore the two parties increase their satisfaction, with no third party being slighted.

Trade favors peaceful relationships between men and contributes to the moral enhancement of these relationships, since for the exchanges to be efficient, they have to exclude lying. In societies of any degree of complexity, trading requires confidence. Many examples are given in Alain Peyrefitte's book La Societé de Confiance (The Confident Society) Editions Odile Jacob, 1995.

When men are free to make their exchanges, the best products and decisions carry the day in all spheres of human action. It follows that free exchange raises continuously the living standards and the thinking of all who participate in it. Sad to say, in the world we live in, much trade is not free. The State intervenes massively to control and tax our exchanges, indeed, even to ban them. This may be for reasons of pure ideology, as in the case of the fixing of minimum salaries or doctors' fees. It may be to defend particular interest groups or particular occupations which have electoral importance, as in the case of Customs duties or import quotas. Or it might even be to forestall public disturbances, as in the case of demands by the militant unions.

Historically, two men are particularly famous for promoting free trade between nations: the Englishman Richard Cobden, and the Frenchman Frédéric Bastiat. These were two great economists, but also, and most importantly, men with profound ethical convictions.

In Manchester in 1838, Richard Cobden and John Bright set up the Anti-Corn Law League, whose initial objective was the abolition of the laws limiting the importation of wheat, laws against the interests of the people but favorable to the great land-owners. Soon, however, driven at once by a remarkable understanding of economic phenomena and great sympathy for the suffering of the population, they took as their target the total and unilateral abolition of protectionism.

For seven years they organized meetings, lectures and debates from one end of the Kingdom to the other. They published books and pamphlets which sold in their thousands. Then they succeeded, by dint of their original ideas and their tenacity, in getting a large number of people favorable to their ideas elected to Parliament. The Tory government resisted for some years, until a terrible famine in 1845 led the Prime Minister, Robert Peel, to free the importation of grain. This was the first victory. The battle continued in Parliament, and on the 25th June, 1846, unilateral free trade became the law of the land. It was to last 85 years, and gave birth to a brilliant period of freedom and prosperity – the Victorian Age.

In France this movement went unnoticed until Bastiat discovered it by chance. He made it known to his fellow-countrymen in his book Cobden and the League (Cobden et la Ligue) and he tried to launch a comparable movement in France, alas with much less success. At this time, despite two revolutions, the French were already proving much less mature than the English in matters bearing on freedom. We still retain something of Bastiat's efforts, however, in the form of the French Manifesto of the Association for Free Trade (L'Association pour la Liberté des Echanges), written in 1846.

"TRADE is a natural right, just as PROPERTY is. Any citizen who has created or acquired a product must have the option of either using it himself immediately or of selling it to someone else anywhere in the world who agrees to give him in exchange something he wants. To deprive him of this right when his use of it is in no way contrary to public order and decent behavior, solely to satisfy the convenience of some other citizen, is both to legitimate theft and to offend against the law of justice.

It is also to violate the maintenance of order, for what kind of order can exist in a society in which each enterprise , with the assistance of the law and public enforcement, can pursue success by crushing all the others?

It is to fail to recognize the Providential intention that governs human destiny, which is revealed in the infinite variety of climates, seasons, natural forces and individual aptitudes, gifts that God has distributed so unequally among men with the sole aim of uniting them through trade and through the bonds of universal fraternity.

It is to run counter to the development of public prosperity, since anyone who is not free to exchange is not free to choose his work, and is constrained to employ his efforts, his capacities and his capital, as well as the means that nature has placed at his disposal, in a direction unnatural to him..

Finally it is to compromise the peace between nations, for it is to disrupt the relationships that unite them and which will in time make wars impossible by making them too costly."

Association for Free Trade

It is valuable to note in modern terms that when the State interferes with free trade in the marketplace, it usually sides with the producers and against the consumers (the "people"). Why? The votes of the politicians are more easily "bought" by the small group of rich producers who can easily pour money into their re-election campaigns. The same principle applies to the unions' control of politicians. The politicians oblige by passing anti-free-trade "fair wages" and "closed shop" laws to ensure that the unions' members (also the "producers" in this case) win benefits at the expense of their employers (the "consumers"). If this is confusing, just follow the money. In a market, the consumers pay money to buy the goods or services of the producers. A labor union is thus simply another form of producer cartel, like the OPEC oil cartel which keeps the price of oil artificially high - to the detriment of consumers worldwide.

This text of the 1848 Manifesto of the Association for Free Trade is still topical. The battles in favor of free trade are never definitively won. As we will confirm in Chapter 5. free trade is always favorable to consumers and unfavorable to producers, but the latter have more influence politically, as we will explore further in Chapter 21.

Chapter 7. Society and Association

The search for means of cooperation between men imposed from above is a chimera. Since time immemorial, however ,men have discovered, spontaneously, ways of bringing about a cooperative social order, in the absence of which civilizations would long since have vanished, in the war waged by clans seeking to impose their own conceptions of the common good.

Pascal Salin[1]

As we saw in Chapter 4, the individual seeks to cooperate with others in order to attain objectives going beyond his individual capacities. This gives rise to benevolent associations or companies. Some associations last long enough only to complete a specific project, for example, a church fête, and so need no formal structure. They can also have permanent objectives, however, for example cultural or charitable ones. In this case they have formal constitutions and live by subscriptions and endowments. At least they would in free societies. But in the one we live in, the State (and local government) blight this intention in two ways:

- In a way that likes to see itself as edifying, by the giving of special benefits to associations over individuals This practice is immoral. We can show why with a concrete example. If in a particular district people set up an association for playing football, there is no valid reason for making people who do not like football support this activity with money extorted from them by means of local taxes. This is not, however, the worst of it. Let's assume that the community is split between lovers of football and lovers of basketball. One might be naïve enough to think that the football-lovers might give money to the football club and the basketball supporters might give some to the basketball club. But politicians are more artful than that. The mayor will raise money by taxing all the locals and then blow his own trumpet about how he's supporting both these associations financially. This will cost the community more, since part of the money raised will have to cover the administrative costs of the tax collection and redistribution. Even then we have to hope that a further fraction of these

---

1   *Libéralisme*, Editions Odile Jacob, 2000.

funds won't be diverted into other uses. It's possible that no one will pay any attention to the resulting increase in levies, and if someone criticizes it once, this will soon be forgotten, whereas the mayor will get himself applauded at every football and basketball game.

- The State (and local government) also impair the liberal scheme of things in a shameful way by financing associations which have no purpose except to get tax monies for their cronies, or get around their limits of employment, or reduce their formal budgets. In France the funds thus spent by the various ministries are of the order of a billion Euros. For the most part they finance semipublic organizations under government tutelage and run by functionaries. These excesses are often reported by the "Cour des Comptes", the administration auditing the State expenses, but even the publication of such audits seem not to trouble the people in power in the least.

In the past one of the most useful roles of the associations was mutual help in the face of the unforeseen contingencies of life. Mutual Aid Societies have always existed in one form or another. After a brief eclipse during the French Revolution, they experienced a rapid growth from the beginning of Napoleon's First Empire, under the influence of the Philanthropic society of Paris, which had been founded as far back as 1780, by the most eminent members of the liberal nobility. This Society declared in 1806 that "It is a question of getting the workers to link up for their mutual assurance of resources in cases of illness, or of those in which the infirmities of old age make it impossible for them to continue in their employment". This mutual assistance was thus advanced as an alternative to aid, which signifies dependency and affronts individual dignity. Mutual assistance, resting on freely agreed efforts at saving, tends on the contrary to encourage responsibility in the individual, who takes personal charge of his own saving. In the event, the example swiftly became widespread.

Similarly, Benjamin Franklin in 1752 co-founded the Philadelphia Contributionship for the Insurance of Houses from Loss by Fire - the first mutual fire insurance company in America. Seven years later, Franklin was also instrumental in getting the first life insurance company, the Presbyterian Ministers' Fund, off the ground.

"I witnessed the spontaneous apparition of Mutual Aid Societies" Bastiat tells in 1848, " more than twenty-five years ago among the most destitute workers and artisans in the poorest villages of the department of the Landes.

The aim of these societies is obviously to achieve a general leveling of the sense of satisfaction, the spreading over all the periods in life of the pay received in the good days. In all the locations in which they exist, they have done a huge amount of good. The members felt buoyed up by a feeling of security, one of the most precious and reassuring sentiments that can accompany man on his pilgrimage here below. What is more, they are all aware of their dependence on each other and how useful they are to each other and they understand the extent to which the ups and downs of each individual or job become common ups and downs. They come together for a few religious ceremonies provided for in their statutes. In a word they are called upon to exercise over each other that vigilant watch so useful in its inspiring self-respect and at the same time a feeling of human dignity, the first and difficult rung on the ladder of all civilization.

What has been at the root of the success of these societies up to now, a success that is slow, in truth, like everything that involves the masses, is freedom- something that speaks for itself.

Their natural pitfall is in the loss of responsibility. Relieving individuals of the consequences of their own actions is never without the risk of creating great dangers and problems for the future. The day on which all citizens might say to themselves "We are paying a subscription to help those who are unable to work or who cannot find work", it is to be feared that we will see developing to a dangerous degree people's natural inclination to inertia and that soon those who are hardworking will be reduced to being the dupes of those who are lazy. Mutual assistance therefore implies mutual surveillance, without which the funds in question would be rapidly exhausted. This reciprocal surveillance, which is a guarantee of existence for the association and a certainty that he is not being duped for each associate member, moreover constitutes the true moral basis for the institution. Thanks to it, drunkenness and debauchery are gradually disappearing, for what right would someone have to the help of the common fund who can be proved to have deliberately courted illness and unemployment by his own fault and as a result of depraved habits? It is this surveillance that restores the Responsibility whose incentive tended to be weakened by the very nature of association.

Well, for this surveillance to take place and bear fruit Friendly Societies have to be free, circumscribed and masters of both their statutes and their funds. They have to be able to vary their rules to suit the requirements of each location[2].

Throughout its history, mutual insurance has been prey to interference by the State.

In 1848 Bastiat was already alarmed because a Commission of the Legislative Assembly had been charged with preparing a Bill with regard to Friendly Societies. In a famous text, now serving as an anthology piece for liberals, especially with doctors, he explained the perils of this interference:

Let us suppose that the government intervenes. It is easy to guess the role it will take upon itself. Its first care will be to take control of all the funds on the pretext of centralizing them, and in order to prettify that purpose it will promise to increase them through resources taken from taxpayers. "For", it will say, "Is it not only natural and just that the State should contribute to such a great, generous, philanthropic and humanitarian task?" The first injustice is its forcing its way into the society by means of subscriptions from citizens who ought not to be contributing to this allocation of assistance. Next, on the pretext of unity or solidarity (or whatever), it will plan to merge all the associations into one single one, subject to a uniform set of rules.

But, I ask, what will have become of the moral status of the institution when its funds are supplied by taxation, when nobody, other than some bureaucrat or other, will have an interest in defending the common fund, when each person, instead of considering it his duty to prevent any abuses, will take a delight in encouraging them, when all mutual surveillance will have ceased and feigning an illness will be nothing other than playing a good trick on the government? The government, to do it justice, is willing to defend itself, but as it can no longer count on private action, it has to substitute public action for it. It will nominate auditors, controllers and inspectors. Countless formalities will come between need and assistance In short, an admirable institution will be transformed into a department of the police.

---

2   *Economic Harmonies*, 1848

In the first instance, the State will see only the advantage of expanding the set of its creatures, increasing the number of sinecures it awards and extending its patronage and electoral influence. It will not see that by allocating to itself a new function it has taken on a new responsibility, and I will go as far as to say that this responsibility is terrifying. For what will be the immediate result? Workers will no longer see the common fund as a property that they administer, contribute to and whose limits circumscribe their rights. Gradually they will come to see assistance in the case of illness or unemployment not as coming from a limited fund instigated by their own foresight but as a debt owed them by Society. They will not accept that it may be impossible to finance and will never be happy with its allocations. The State will constantly be constrained to ask for subsidies from the budget. At this point, when it encounters opposition from the Finance Commissioners, it will find itself in inextricable difficulty. Abuses will constantly increase and rectification will be postponed from year to year, as is the usual thing, until one day an explosion occurs. But when this happens, it will be apparent that the authorities are reduced to dealing with a population that no longer knows how to act for itself, that expects everything, even subsistence, to be provided by ministers and prefects and whose ideas will have been warped to the extent that they have lost any notion of Law, Property, Freedom and Justice[3].

This text was pure premonition. A century later, in 1945, the State finally stripped mutual aid of its essential functions by creating Social Security and what Bastiat had described is exactly what came to pass.

---

3   *Economic Harmonies*, 1848

Chapter 8. Business

Business...is no more than a collection of contracts...Just as any contract is an instrument of peaceful social cooperation, business too is a coming-together of peaceful social cooperation.
Pascal Salin[1]

Business is just a special case of what we dealt with in the previous chapter, namely association. It is an association to which some people bring capital (savings) and others bring their labor.

A business rests on contracts. It starts off with someone (the businessman or entrepreneur) thinking that somewhere in society there is an unexploited demand waiting to be met, one he has insufficient means to satisfy on his own. So he sets up a business and convinces various people to supply him with resources, by persuading them that the sale of the goods or services produced by the business will create a certain return on these resources. Such payments may be tied to the results achieved (in which case they are called dividends and those who accept this kind of risk are called shareholders), or they may be laid down in advance (in which they are called interest payments and those who earn them are called lenders). These participants are mutually bound by contracts. The business is then in a position to organize other contracts, notably with those who are going to contribute their labor to it.

For example, consider Apple Computer. Steve Jobs is the entrepreneur, the business entity is Apple and a product that Jobs thought would fulfill an unexploited demand is the iPad.

In the Third Part of this book, we will examine business enterprise in relation to its economic aspects. In the present chapter we will look at its social aspects, not without noting, however, that two economists, Frédéric Bastiat in his day[2], and Pascal Salin in our times[3], have produced the most

---

1 *Libéralisme*
2 *Economic Harmonies* (Chapter on Earnings)
3 *Libéralisme* (Chapter on Business); *The Firm in a Free Society* (*Journal of Libertarian Studies* Summer 2002 issue) – this paper was presented to the Conference to mark the bicentenary of the birth of Bastiat, organised by the Cercle Frédéric Bastiat, in 2001. It is available in English on the Cercle's website, www.bastiat.net.

subtle and profound analyses on the subject. We have borrowed some ideas from them in what follows.

Bastiat shows, historically, how it was that associations were open to the idea of transforming themselves into business enterprises. The process begins with the evolution of mutual aid societies, whose aim was to cover the risks which life presents by means of subscriptions. From one year to the next, this subscription can vary in terms of the more or the less great incidence of materialized risk. The association therefore diminishes unforeseen risks, but it does not eliminate them. We can see in this circumstance that an entrepreneur who manages to interest a sufficient number of individuals for him to be able to make reliable probability calculations, will be in a position to offer them fixed subscriptions. In this way the insurance company is born. It enables insured people to remain in the association without worrying too much about it.

The wage-earning class is born from the same desire to eliminate risk. Bastiat gives the example of an experienced hunter who takes a youth into his service. He can equally well share the successes with him or take the risks himself, which his experience makes it possible for him to do, and give a fixed payment to his companion. The latter will enjoy security, he himself sole power of decision.

Bastiat next shows us that the alliance between those who bring their savings to the enterprise and those who bring their labor to it, brings to each one advantages which he could not otherwise enjoy.

An old fisherman says one day to his friend: "You have neither a boat, nor nets nor any tool other than your hands with which to fish, and you are running a great risk of having a very poor catch. You do not have any supplies either, and yet you cannot work on an empty stomach. Come with me; it is in your interest just as it is in mine. It is in yours, for I will give you part of our catch, and whatever it is it will always be more profitable to you than what you catch single-handed. It is also in my interest, for any extra catch resulting from your help will exceed the share I will have to give you. In a word, the combination of your and my work and my capital will make us more compared to what each of these would achieve in isolation, and it is the share of this excess that explains how an association between us can be beneficial to both."

And this is what happened. Later the young fisherman preferred to receive a fixed quantity of fish each day. His random profit was thus converted into a wage without requiring the formation of a formal association.

In joining up in a common endeavor, capital and labor therefore satisfy two tendencies we find in varying degree among all men: unity of purpose and constant income. Business enterprise is therefore truly in its essence a peaceful cooperation. All parties benefit.

"This is why", Pascal Salin tells us, "we should shed those reflexes that decades of latent Marxism have instilled in our minds, reflexes which lead us to an antagonistic view of social relationships, and in turn to the view that enterprise and labor are enemies and that the one can gain only by imposing a loss on the other. In this, the major intellectual error of our era, there is a twofold ignorance: we forget that all wealth is created, and is not a payment from some mysterious pre-existing source. We forget that a contract does not include one loser and one winner, but two winners. Business enterprise, a set of contracts and therefore of social cooperation, is necessarily a source of the creation of wealth to the advantage of all the partners.

Firms can be efficient only if the workers in them are content. The major preoccupation of any good businessman is to act in such a way that this will be the case. This is very difficult, for each one of us complacently imagines that his merits are never sufficiently appreciated, and union bosses incite us to think this way. In private enterprise it is often achieved, however, because unionization stands at only 5% today in France, and it is common to find union members themselves discreetly asking for a place in the firm for their children. In the U.S., unions account for less than 15% of the private sector workforce. In the public sector, bosses have guaranteed careers (the "civil service") and are less interested in their subordinates. From this there derives a latent discontent, much stronger unionization and recurrent strikes, for which the clients (taxpayers?) and the country have to pay.

Chapter 9. The Principle of Subsidiarity

Subsidiarity entails privatization and decentralization. Families, voluntary associations and private business are better than the state. (This is privatization). In the public domain, the local village is better than the department, the department is better than the region, and the region is better than the State. (This is decentralization)
Jean-Yves Naudet[1]

Just as individuals associate with their fellows to achieve ends beyond their personal capacities, voluntary associations and private companies link up in various ways to form bigger outfits able to accomplish objectives which none of the individual units could do on its own. There are many associations and companies which operate on this basis in civil society. In this way insurance companies have their largest risks underwritten by companies with very substantial assets.   There exists a huge "reinsurance" market which enables retail insurance companies to pass off some of their own risks to even bigger companies in payment of a small reinsurance premium.

The principle of "subsidiarity", which liberals hold dear, wants this action undertaken by delegation of the powers of individual associations to the group associations. If liberals are wary about this, it is because the tendency of human organizations is more readily in the opposite direction, with the federations themselves fixing policy. In a group of firms it often happens that the largest company often decides, unilaterally, what the smaller units will do.

For example, Microsoft sets defacto software standards which other companies follow. The Windows operating system establishes market-based standards, not dictated by government directives.

It is, however, above all with respect to the division of governmental powers within a single nation that liberals want to see the subsidiarity principle applied.

---

1   Article published on the website www.Libres.org on September 29, 2004, under the title "*Préfets: Decentralisation à la française*".

This principle was defined in the Encyclical "Quadragesimo Anno" (In the Fortieth Year) by Pope Pius XI, in 1931:

"Just as the powers of individuals, which they are capable of carrying out on their own initiative, and in their own way, should not be transferred to the community, so also it would be unjust, and would disturb the social order in a very hurtful way, to take away from groups in the lower ranks and entrust to a collective body on a higher level, functions they are in a position to discharge themselves".

"Let governments leave to groups of lower rank, the management of less important business, in which they would be taking on far too many things; they will consequently be able to guarantee more freely, more powerfully, more efficaciously, those functions which belong only to them, because only they can carry them out".

Taking up the same theme in a different form, Frédéric Bastiat wrote in 1849:

"When the government cannot avoid taking over a service that ought to be the responsibility of the private sector, its discharge should at least be left as close as possible to those on whom it naturally falls".

"Thus in the matter of foundlings, since in principle the father and mother ought to bring the children up, the law must exhaust every possible means of making it so. Failing parents, it should be the village; failing the village, the department. Do you wish to multiply, infinitely, the numbers of foundlings? Declare it the business of the state".

The Swiss Confederation, made up of 23 cantons, is organized on this basis. Its constitution is worded thus:

"The cantons are sovereign, inasmuch as their sovereignty is not limited by the Federal Constitution, and as such they exercise all rights not delegated to the Federal Government. "

The most important word in this text is 'delegated'. All power exercised by the Federal Government is delegated by the cantons.

The best known example of a constitutional recognition of subsidiarity is found in the US Constitution's Bill of Rights. Amendments 9 and 10 reserve those powers not formally granted to the Federal Government to the individual states or citizens.

The principle of subsidiarity made a striking reappearance during the discussion of the European Union's Maastricht Treaty. Its Article 3 is couched as follows.

"In the domains which are not a matter of its exclusive jurisdiction, the Community intervenes, in accordance with the rule of subsidiarity, only if and to the extent that the purposes of the action envisaged, cannot be sufficiently achieved by the member States and can therefore, in view of the scale and difficulty of the action envisaged, be more satisfactorily accomplished at the Community level"..

We are forced to note that reality has never been in line with expectations, so that it is often said maliciously that the European Community uses the principle in the opposite direction: it leaves to the nations only those items it cannot deal with. Nor should we be surprised. Like any constituted body, the European Commission (the executive arm of the E.U., it's "White House") has a tendency to augment its powers under its own steam, but it is also pushed on by the fantasies of this or that head of state. Judging by the enormous extent of the powers the Treaty gives the European Commission, Maastricht rightly frightened the liberals. This is why they strove to introduce the principle of subsidiarity as a safeguard in the EU "Constitution".

Chapter 10. The State

When unlimited and unrestricted by individual rights, a government is man's deadliest enemy. It is not protection against private actions, but against governmental actions that the Bill of Rights was written.

Ayn Rand[1]

The State is an institution which holds the power to put into effect, by force, certain rules of conduct in a given geographical area. In democratic societies, these rules are voted in by a majority of elected representatives. In others the rules are decreed by the government in place. In both cases the State can uphold them through its monopoly on the use of force.

It is clear that if everyone on earth followed liberal moral principles, there would be no need for the State. This is why there exists a small group of liberals, the anarcho-capitalists (and many "libertarians"), who advocate the abolition, pure and simple, of the State. The most famous is the late Murray Rothbard, but they also count among their number famous names like David Friedman (the son of Milton), and in France Bertrand Lemennicier. Of course all the liberals, including, naturally, the anarcho-capitalists, are well aware that if man can acquire wealth by effort and reason, he can also acquire them at the expense of others, particularly by violence. They recognize therefore that a mechanism is needed, whereby the freedom and property of others will be respected. The anarcho-capitalists, however, think that this function can be discharged by private law-courts and police forces, as is already happening more and more anyway. Robert Nozick has shown in rigorous fashion, and Ayn Rand more intuitively, however, that such agencies could not ensure the safety of all, for in the case of conflict between agencies, there would be no regulatory mechanism such as to secure convergence towards single solutions. A single, unique authority would therefore still be necessary.

Most liberals do not even think to pose the question. They hold that the State is necessary, but in the shape of a limited State, one confined

---

1 Capitalism, the Unknown Ideal, 1966

solely to those higher order prerogatives – justice, police and National Defense – which imply international relations. Furthermore they would view these functions as properly exercised under the rule of subsidiarity. The State would constitute a higher order association to which associations on a lower level, such as districts, delegated certain of their prerogatives and resources, somewhat on the lines of what happens in Switzerland. This was the original vision of the American founding fathers.

This is how Bastiat explains the role of the State in The Law:

"Each one of us clearly holds from nature, from God, the right to defend his person, his freedom and his property, since these are the three constitutive and conserving factors in one's life, factors which are mutually fulfilling, and cannot be understood separately. For what are our Faculties but an extension of our Personality, and what is Property other than an extension of our faculties?

If each man has the right to protect his Person, his Freedom and his Property, even by force, then groups of men have the right to consult among themselves, to come to agreements and to organize a communal Force to provide for this defense on a regular basis.

Collective rights, therefore, have their basis, their raison d'être, their legitimacy, in individual rights; and communal force has no other purpose, no other mission than the separate individual forces which it replaces.

Thus just as an individual may not employ force against the Person, Liberty or Property of another individual, for the same reason communal power cannot be legitimately applied to destroy the Person, Liberty or Property of individuals or classes.

For this perversion of power, in one case or the other, would be in contradiction to our premises. Who will presume to say that the power has been given to us not to protect our Rights but to eliminate the equal rights of our fellows? And if this is not so of individual force acting in isolation, how can it be true of collective power, which is only the organized conflation of isolated powers? So if one thing is obvious, it is this: The Law is the organization of the natural Right of legitimate defense. It is the substitution of collective Power for individual powers, in order for it to act in the circle where the latter have the right to act, to do what they have the right to do, in order to guarantee persons, freedom and property, to maintain each person's rights, and secure interpersonal Justice for all[2]."

Now, if a nation existed on such a basis, it seems to me that order would prevail in fact as much as in the mind. It seems to me that the people would have the most simple government, as well as the most economic and the least heavy-handed, the least intrusive, the least managerial, the fairest and therefore the most soundly based one could imagine, whatever its particular political shape.

I say this because, under such a regime, each person would understand clearly that he commanded all the fullness of his life, as well as responsibility for it. Provided that the person is respected, that work may be freely undertaken and its fruits protected against all unjust encroachment, no one would have any quarrel with the state. We would not when we were successful wish to thank the state for it, it is true; but neither would we put the blame on it for our misfortunes, any more than the peasants do with regard to hail or frost. We would recognize in the state the inestimable benefit of security.

The idea of entrusting the State with the protection of our rights, has, nevertheless, something paradoxical about it, for the historical record of the immoral actions States have engaged in, has vastly outperformed those of private criminals. Year after year, the reports of Amnesty International are full of the horrors perpetrated by governments: wars, deportations, concentration camps, destruction and abduction, arbitrary detention, torture, famine, persecution, murder, and property confiscation.

The State is the greatest potential danger for the individual, for it holds the "legal" monopoly on the use of force and this attracts power-mad men like so many flies. These men aspire to direct society and any individual action seems to them potentially deviant and therefore dangerous. They simply cannot, therefore, be "liberals". The only way of limiting the damage these sociopaths do is to restrict their powers very severely by appropriate institutions - checks and balances. This is why liberals have evolved the principle of the separation of powers, so difficult to get to operate, even in our old democracy. It was the liberals who invented the "Bill of Rights"

---

2   Capital and bold letters were used by Bastiat exactly as they are reproduced here.

in England in 1689 and in America in 1791[3]. In France, "La Déclaration des Droits de l'Homme et du Citoyen" was adopted at the initiative of Lafayette during the early phase of the French Revolution, the liberal one. But the Jacobins ignored it and promoted instead the "Terror", which was to become the matrix of all subsequent totalitarian states. It was reinstated from the Second Republic (1848) on.

---

3   In the United States, The "Bill of Rights" is another name given to the first ten Amendments adopted in 1791 to the Constitution of 1789.

Chapter 11. The Rights of Man

The rights of man did not begin with the French Revolution. They go back to the Judeo- Christian tradition which proclaimed the importance of the individual and the sacred character of the human person and of certain individual rights which no government can take away. Next we had the Magna Carta of 1215, the articulation of rights in the seventeenth Century and our peaceful revolution of 1688, when Parliament imposed its will on the monarchy.

Margaret Thatcher

With these words Margaret Thatcher reminds us that, historically, the "rights of man" were conceived as a protection of the individual against the customary coercion of the State. The American Declaration of Independence, three years before the French Declaration of the Rights of Man and the Citizen was based on the same idea:

"We hold these truths to be self-evident, that all men are created equal, that they are endowed by their Creator with certain unalienable Rights, that among these are Life, Liberty and the pursuit of Happiness. — That to secure these rights, Governments are instituted among Men, deriving their just powers from the consent of the governed, — That whenever any Form of Government becomes destructive of these ends, it is the Right of the People to alter or to abolish it, and to institute new Government, laying its foundation on such principles and organizing its powers in such form, as to them shall seem most likely to effect their Safety and Happiness".

The French Declaration of the Rights of Man and the Citizen of 1789 and the American Bill of Rights introduced as amendments to the U.S. Constitution in 1791 embrace essentially the same reasoning. They guaranteed freedom of speech, movement and religion, they guaranteed property, security and equality before the law. These are the "rights to do" things without being harassed by the state.

However, from 1793 another category of rights, so-called "economic and social rights", was introduced in the Subsequent Declarations. These rights were no longer "rights to do" things, but rather "rights to obtain" things, such as education, or a dwelling place or a job, without its being specified which entity must procure this something or which body be sanctioned if this something be not obtained.

In practice the enunciation of these pseudo-rights to this or that thing, signifies that it is to the State that the duty of procuring it for everyone has been delegated, a task it will obviously not be able to undertake short of a redistribution of resources obtained by coercion. Any new right "to" something, which naïve people will think is progress, is actually a blank check to the State, a further step in the creep towards totalitarianism. These rights are therefore incompatible with that liberal morality and philosophy of the state which we defined in the last chapter.

The downward drift began with the very first years of the French Revolution, for while the liberals formed a majority on the Commission which drafted the Declaration of 1789, the Jacobins kept their wits about them and poisoned the actual outcome. In Chapter 1.1.we directed the reader's admiration to the formulation of Article 4 of the Declaration: "Freedom consists in being able to do everything which does not harm other people; thus the exercise of natural rights has no limits other than those which assure to other members of society the enjoyment of these same rights".

The moment has come to confess that the quotation was not complete. Article 4 continues in fact as follows: "These limits can be determined only by the Law". In this way the Jacobins managed to sneak in through the window a State for which the liberals had refused to open the door.

Other articles are marked by the same base deceit. For example, Article 10: "No one must be harassed as to his opinions, not even his religious ones, provided that their expression does not offend against the public order established by the Law". Article 3 is even worse. "The basis of all sovereignty lies essentially in the Nation. No corporate body and no individual can exercise any authority which does not expressly emanate from it".

But we should not be too punctilious. This Declaration stresses no other rights than Liberty, property, safety, and resistance to oppression. It limits the power than the State could arrogate to itself in order to guarantee these rights. Its principal purpose is to protect the individual against the arbitrariness of the State. In this acceptance, it has been an absolute progress. We reproduce it as an appendix to this chapter in order to allow the reader to judge for himself.

The first of the "rights to obtain" figured in the Declaration of 1793, the preamble to the Constitution of the so called Year I, which adds some supplementary ones to the Declaration of 1789, including the following: "Society must provide for the subsistence of citizens in distress, whether by obtaining work for them, or in guaranteeing the means of subsistence for those not in a fit state to work" (Article 21). Or another example: "Everybody needs education. Society must do everything in its power to promote the progress of public enlightenment, and bring education within the reach of all citizens" (Article 22).

This Declaration had the same ephemeral life as the Constitution it preceded, but in the on-going chain of constitutions, other declarations were to see the light of day, in a varying mixture of "rights to do" and "rights to obtain".

The preamble to the French Constitution of 1946 includes the right to a job and a free education, such as to ensure for the individual and his family "the conditions necessary to their development", guaranteeing to all "the protection of health, security, rest and leisure". The present French Constitution, which dates from 4 October 1958, contains in the preamble the Liberal Declaration of 1789, but also the Statist preamble of the Constitution of 1946, a schizophrenic sequence which explains in part the incapacity of the State to take simple and rational decisions.

The Universal Declaration of the Rights of Man issued by the United Nations Organization in 1948 comprises two sorts of articles. The first twenty are quite satisfactory from the liberal point of view: they protect real, individual rights. They are akin to the U.S. Bill of Rights.

However, the ten items following belong to the "rights to obtain" category, largely inspired by the Preamble to the French Constitution of 1946, René Cassin having initially drafted both projects. These ten are more duties of the State than individual Rights. This explains why Article 25.1 declares that: "All individuals have the right to a standard of living sufficient to ensure their and their family's health and well-being, especially in regard to food, clothing, housing and medical needs, as well as for necessary social services; they also have a right to security in case of unemployment or sickness, invalidity, widowhood, old age or other cases of the loss of the means of subsistence, as a result of circumstances outside their control".

The effect of the addition of these egregiously vague pieties, without its being specified either who is to put them into effect or what sanctions are to be applied in the case of non-compliance, is substantially to weaken the impact of this kind of text. Of course we understand that the idea is for the State to get all this going, but it is quite clear that most of the signatory States do not have the capacity to carry this out. What exactly is a "sufficient standard of living?" What would the international tribunal do if an action were brought before it against a state with 10% unemployment, like France? The trouble is that enfeebling that part of the text means weakening all of it. This, indeed, is precisely what the totalitarian states wanted, given that they were not in the least enamored with the first twenty articles. During the vote on this Declaration, on 20 December 1948, the totalitarian states abstained….because they judged that the number of articles dealing with economic and social "rights" had been cut back too much!

"A collectivist tyranny," says Ayn Rand, "does not have the audacity to reduce a country to slavery by the immediate confiscation of all it has of value, material and moral. It acts by a process of internal corruption. In the same way as a country is stripped of its wealth by means of inflation, inflation is employed to deprive people of their rights. The process involves such a promiscuous enunciation of new rights that the people do not notice that the meaning of the concept is being turned upside down. Just as bad money chases away good, so these meretricious rights destroy real ones.

It is remarkable that there has never been, anywhere in the world, such a   proliferation, simultaneously, of two apparently contradictory phenomena: so-called "new rights" and labor camps.

Appendix A presents the Bill of Rights of the Constitution of the United States ratified by the American States on December 15, 1791.

Appendix B presents the Declaration of the Rights of Man and of the Citizen approved by the National Assembly of France on August 26, 1789.

Chapter 12. Justice, Rights and the Law

The Law is the enemy of natural rights. Legal is the enemy of legitimate. Legal positivism is the enemy of justice. Natural rights, whose essential task is to permit peaceful and fruitful cooperation between men, in protecting property and contracts, have been diverted from that mission, in decades, by a bogus law which functions like an instrument of political will, not only of the majoritarian kind, which would be tyranny enough, but more and more of oligarchies and pressure groups who have de facto taken over the power of the state.

Philippe Nemo[1]

"Law is justice," so Bastiat tells us several times in his famous pamphlet The Law. This aphorism may have a hazy edge for the modern reader, given the many senses which the word "Justice" embraces today. Things were not like this in 1850, when the word "justice" meant "Moral virtue which leads to the rendering to each person of what is rightfully his and to the rights of others being respected". (Dictionnaire Bescherelle 1970).

Among the different definitions that we find in the Petit Larousse today, two will still find favor with the liberal:

A moral principle which demands respect for rights and for fairness, and

An action by which a government or legal authority recognizes the rights of each person.

However, in the same dictionary, you'll also find the definition of "social justice" dear to socialists:

Which demands equitable conditions of life for each person, meaning roughly, in the socialist world-view, the same final incomes after redistribution for all, (with the unofficial exception of those who run the government, of course).

---

1   Preface to Patrick Simon's book *Natural Law and its Friends* and Enemies (François-Xavier Guibert, 2005. This book is a survey which by way of a very enjoyable read yields a deeper understanding of the very rich notion of natural law, an idea dear to liberals but unknown or scorned by socialists.

In the face of concrete circumstances, most individuals understand from the core of their being, a clear concept of what is just and unjust.

Liberal philosophy and socialist philosophy are fundamentally opposed on this question of "justice", as they are on the question of "solidarity" with which we deal in the next chapter.

To sum up: for the liberal, justice is the application of natural law, and actual law is the simplest translation of this same natural law into codified texts which regulate life in society, a kind of set of directions for the application of that natural law.

In English-language countries, the concept of "common law: describes this natural understanding perfectly.

For the socialist there is no natural law. Rather it is legislation which imposes law in order to make men "better" according to the criteria of those in power, if need be against their will. As Saint-Just puts it: "The legislator commands the future. It is for him to will what is good. It is for him to make men what he wants them to be".

Roman Law and the "civil law" that has followed is a logical development of this understanding.

Patrick Simon gives us this definition of natural law: "It is the rules of right behavior which men practice spontaneously or discover. On the other hand, imperative legislation, from which one cannot deviate, is expressed in the imposition of artificial rules. To emphasize the point and to make oneself clearly understood, one can say that natural law is often justice, and that decreed law is often force".[2]

Patrick Simon, developing this idea so dear to liberals, with all his customary explanatory skill, strives to show that there are two types of law: the spontaneous kind which we discover in ourselves, and the legislative kind which is imposed. His experience as a maritime lawyer, lends a special gravity to his interpretations, since on the high seas the dealings between ship-owners and crews elude the laws of nations, and yet over the centuries laws have emerged and become established. As long ago as 1996, Patrick

---

2   Ibid.

Simon presented a superb synthesis in this regard to the Frederic Bastiat Circle, from which we are borrowing a great deal in the lines which follow.[3]

For most of our compatriots, used to centuries of dirigisme, the law is legislation, that is to say something imposed from outside. In reality, legislation is only the visible part of law and not necessarily the most useful. The most important element is that which is not seen, but which is practiced every day and comes from within. The case is a bit like morality. For a child morality consists in irritating interdictions.. The child does not yet understand that morality belongs to personal choice and comes from within himself As Hayek puts it, "men who have enunciated a rule have not created it, they have voiced it".

The freely negotiated contract is the expression par excellence of spontaneous law. In a contract the parties tentatively seek out some expression of their agreement satisfactory to both sides. In a contract each signatory is obliged to take account of the wishes of the others.

A contract is not necessarily written. Millions of dealings between individuals are regulated by tacit agreements to which the law gives precise form only in the case of conflict brought before a court. Law bases itself on good sense and becomes more refined in the light of experience. It is in all truth , therefore, substantially a matter of progressive discovery and not of creation ex nihilo.

It is not necessary that each precise case have been already dealt with by a court in order for a case-law judgment to be made in its respect. On the contrary we can imagine the insane dimensions of a code which would classify individual cases in detail. In fact, however, something like this is what does happen today. The mania for legislating on each and every activity strikes at very many people and situations. There are in France something of the order of 90 codes each containing between several hundred and several thousand pages! The U.S. Code of Federal Regulations, or CFR, runs to many dozens of feet in length, Every citizen is bound by its laws. This obviously renders impossible the application of the rule "no one is supposed to ignore the law" , a rule which is nevertheless logically indispensable to the peaceful functioning of a society.

---

3   A review of this can be found on the site www.bastiat.net, in the section, "les textes des précédents dîners-débâts.

One of the reasons for this expansion is without doubt the increased complexity of society, resulting basically from technical progress, but the main reason is explained by a school of Economic thought known as "Public Choice" whose leading light is the Nobel Prize winner in Economics, American James Buchanan.[4] In the political market, according to this school, politicians exchange favors for votes. While these favors benefit an identifiable group, however, their costs get buried in the mass of obligatory contributions.

Patrick Simon's witty explanation of some of the findings of this school is in terms of a ménage à trois, whose actors are: a) the politician, b) the voter and c) the third party taxpayer - in this event, the cuckold.

The politician looks for votes from the most numerous groups of supporters by promising them benefits and advantages. He has no money of his own to spend, but if elected he will be able to force the less numerous third group to contribute, by his voting for particular legislation.

Patrick Simon gives as examples:

. The various laws on rental agreements, which systematically favor the tenants, who far outnumber the proprietors.
. Labor codes which systematically favor employees (numerous) against the employers who are fewer.
. The dock workers' monopoly, damaging to the ship-owners, most of whom are not French (or American) voters.

In all these cases the law is not based on the search for what is right; it is traded for votes in the political market-place. As though in some inherent and blind process of revenge, however, the law inexorably punishes, not those who voted for it, but the very groups it was supposed to protect. The laws on rent have led to a scarcity of rented accommodations; those laws on work have led to a shortage of jobs. The dock workers' monopoly has entailed the ruin of French ports to the benefit of other European ones. In the United States, similar laws are pending in Congress to establish a new Mexican-US super-highway to enable shippers to use Mexican ports to bypass the uncompetitive US ones. The lawmaker has created false laws: the tenants, workers and dockers thought they had a right, but the

---

4   See Chapter 21 below.

supply which existed before this right shrinks like the skin of the wild ass in Balzac's La Peau de Chagrin.

As long as the law is based on general, universally-agreed principles, so long as it limits itself to defining the limits of good conduct, it is readily assimilated and respected. This is still the case with the Civil Code. When the latter proclaims "Everything which causes harm to other people requires him by whose fault it occurred, to make reparation for it", it does no more than articulate a universally accepted rule as a just command.

When, however, the law penetrates all the details of daily life, or when it favors one particular group, it loses all respectability. Then one sees more and more groups which protest, demonstrate, rage and destroy - with the sole aim of forcibly obtaining advantages from the law-maker, or maintaining those which favor them to the detriment of others.

There is no way this situation can continue indefinitely. It is more and more difficult for the law-maker to devise coherent rules which cover all the new cases which the imagination of man can multiply. In the end, the solution can come only from a diminution in the number of laws known as "imperative" (those binding on all) in favor of those known as "supplementary" (those which are imposed only in the cases where there is no existing contractual agreement between the parties).

This is a bit like what happens today between individuals or societies belonging to different nations. The contracts which they make between themselves, take from each of the national legislations, the clauses which seem to them most useful. In case of disagreement, they appeal to private arbiters chosen by common agreement and specified in the contract. They have no recourse, therefore, to the courts of this or that nation. The European edifice has given a boost to contracts of this kind, which has permitted international jurists to verify the validity of the concepts developed in the chapter.

Throughout the world, private arbitration societies such as the American Arbitration Association in the United States, or the International Arbitration Court (a non-government organization) based in London, England, do much if not most of the conflict resolution between private business entities, bypassing the Nation States' court systems.

Chapter 13. Solidarity

"The same men who, even in direst need would blush for shame at the thought of begging from their neighbors, lose all scruple once the state intervenes, sparing their consciences any direct confrontation with the baseness of such behavior.

Farmers, manufacturers, merchants, ship owners, artists, singers, dancers, men of letters, civil servants of all kinds, businessmen, contractors, bankers – everybody in France demands state handouts.

In order to give these rather abject measures a veneer of authority and regularity, they have all been assimilated to what is known as the "principle of solidarity", a word which, employed thus, means nothing more nor less than the efforts of all the citizens to pillage each other, via the costly intervention of the state".

F. Bastiat[1]

Our dignity as human beings requires that each one of us, once we have passed the stage of infancy, should create at least as many resources as he consumes for his personal needs. This is a principle which education, whether supplied by parents or the school, ought to inculcate in children, and this was once in practice the case, when the sense of individual dignity was an honored and incontestable value. Today complaints and excuses have replaced this sentiment, with the results we see around us.

There are, however, a certain number of human beings, handicapped at birth or by life, who are not capable, any more than children are, to come to terms with their situation. Solidarity – the feeling that we have for our fellow human being – is the moral virtue which is exercised in helping them. One says "helping" advisedly, and not simply "ensuring" their subsistence by the forced anonymous taxation of others. The Olympic Games for Handicapped People demonstrate how great the resources of the human being are, and the handicapped person making a partial contribution to his own subsistence gains much more pride from it than from what we "give" him when he sinks into total dependency on state aid. Children too are much better prepared for life if they take part in household chores, or in voluntary work for the local community, or earn their own pocket-money.

1   *Peace and Liberty: or the Republican Budget* (1848).

Liberals and socialists have completely opposite visions of caring for others. For liberals, the ideas of common humanity and solicitude for one's fellow-men are individual virtues which operate directly or through voluntary associations. This is the kind of togetherness one finds in small communities such as families, villages, neighborhoods and work-places, where people know each other well and get mutually involved. When the need for solidarity goes beyond the circle of parents and personal acquaintances, it is exercised through associations which set themselves concrete objectives and strive to achieve them, which is far more effective than, say, taxes on airfares handed to corrupt tyrants without any real thought as to the uses to which they will be put.

For socialists, concern for one's fellows is realized by getting the state to redistribute monies it has forcefully taken from others. This is obviously without moral value save perhaps to salve consciences. Why help one's neighbor if one is already paying the state to do it?

In practice, the State kills pity, but its false charity allows the men in power to blow their own trumpet. In truth such falsity has become across the years a spider's web so complex that no one can master it anymore, one that leaves the field wide open to iniquity, waste and corruption of all kinds. This is even more true when this pseudo-charity, undertaken by states, is mediated through other states, as in the case of "aid" to poor countries.

Many people, however, ask themselves the following question: if the State did not systematize help to the destitute, would not some unfortunates slip through the mesh of the safety net? Let me offer you a few snippets of reflection on this question.

1. Government based "solidarity" in fact allows many unfortunates to fall through the net. Thus, while over the years, the Gross Domestic Product has never ceased to grow in France, one can no longer walk around Paris or take a simple ride on the Metro, without seeing beggars or people of no fixed abode. In the United States, the so-called "war on poverty" has been waged for over 40 years at a cost approaching a trillion dollars. Yet, the number of people below the official "poverty line" is higher than ever.

2. By contrast, in the French villages in past times, people let no one slip through the net, as all those who lived in a village before World War II will still remember.

We talked earlier about Mutual Aid Societies.[2] Since WWII, Social Security has rendered these societies pointless, both in Francs and the US. Furthermore, in France there have been set up by legislation in all the villages, "Communal Committees for Social Action" (Comités Communaux D'Action Sociale CCAS), which constitute an administrative apparatus, which allows those elected to increase their influence, even to find jobs for their cronies, thus inevitably eliminating what in the past could take the form of real pity for those whom chance had been brought low.

3. In his book, Losing Ground, published in 1984, Charles Murray made a very careful study of the social policy of American government between 1950 and 1980, using indices of rates of poverty, crime, illiteracy, unemployment, drug-use and extra-marital births.

Murray showed that between 1950 and 1965, a market economy in a largely non-interventionist state had considerably reduced the poverty which existed at the end of the war, with all the above indices in decline. From 1965, well-intentioned governments wanted to eliminate such poverty as remained, by means of massive expenditures of the kind the Americans call the "Welfare State", and the French call "l'Etat Providence" (literally, the "Salvation State").[3] These programs have resulted in the aggravation of the undesirable behavior they sought to eliminate and brought an explosion in the incidence of the ills listed above. The help to the unemployed has discouraged many people from working, by rendering unemployment acceptable, financially and socially. The payments made to unmarried mothers have led to a rapid growth in births outside wedlock, and the exploitation of these unfortunate women by unscrupulous men.

Charles Murray also noted that in the previous century, when caring for others was left to private initiative, the portion of their income which individuals devoted to charity was much greater than that donated today when it happens via the State as a coercive intermediary. Even today, however, just as before, money spent privately is more efficient. Every Euro spent in private charity has a return far superior to one spent by

2   In Chapter 7.
3   Contrary to what current misconceptions would lead us to believe, the levels of expenditure on social security in the United States and Western Europe appear to be of the same order when the same categories are considered.

public charity: we are much more careful how money is used when it is ours which is being spent. Organizations like Médecins sans Frontières (Doctors without Boundaries) and Restaurants du Coeur (Restaurants of the Heart)[4] supply all contributors with much more precise information on the use made of their money than the State does about the sums it extorts from us. Philanthropists like Bill and Melinda Gates, who spend some of their fortune in this way, are even more careful about the use made of their donations.

---

4   This French charity distributes food packages and hot meals to needy recipients.

Part Three:

The Economy

Chapter 14. Economic Theories

Political Economy is the science which teaches the workers to guard vigilantly what belongs to them.
Frédéric Bastiat[1]

Part Three is not a course in Economics. Its purpose is to clarify the economic consequences of the rules of individual conduct and of life in society expounded in Parts One and Two. Once again the guiding spirit of our reasoning will be moral, but just as in earlier chapters, we will show the practical, utilitarian advantages of the liberal economy.

The Petit Larousse defines Economic Liberalism as "the economic doctrine of free enterprise, according to which the State should not, by its intervention, compromise the free play of competition". This could not be better expressed. This definition implies more generally the non-intervention of the State in the economy and thus entails "Private property in the means of production and exchange", the sentence which the same Petit Larousse uses to define capitalism. This is a useful distinction, for many people confuse liberalism and capitalism. Capitalism is not liberalism. Capitalism is a sub-set of a liberal economy.

How does the liberal economy fit in with the various economic doctrines the reader may have come across? To answer this question we will begin by defining these doctrines in summary form, spelling out their main characteristics and naming some of the economists attached to them. To enable the non-specialist reader to cope, we have chosen the best known names, without this implying any hierarchy of distinction or value-judgment on our part.

Viewed from afar, economists divide into four schools.[2]

---

1   War against the professorial establishment in Political Economy.
2   Viewed from closer in, things are a bit more complicated, because certain economists like Krugman and Stiglitz, have made contributions to several theoretical schools, and others, like Allais, or Samuelson, have evolved over the course of their careers.

1. The neo-Classical school. its name derives from the fact that the classical school, illustrated for example by the Italian economist Vilfredo Pareto (of "Pareto's Law" fame) and the French economist Léon Walras, underwent a certain eclipse when the Keynesian school was in the ascendant. It revived after the war when Keynesian policies led to stagflation (stagnation combined with inflation). Among its best-known exponents are Milton Friedman in the United States and Maurice Allais in France.

This school employs the traditional scientific method, which consists in formulating hypotheses inspired by observation, and deducing laws from them, either by reasoning or by means of mathematical models, and then in verifying these laws by experiments. The drawback is that economists cannot conduct experiments in many cases. They try therefore, with more or less success, to compare the consequences of these laws with the evidence by using historical data and statistics.

This school seeks improvements in the use of existing resources. Its subject-matter is essentially the individual as a consumer and the firm as a producer. It is behind two very useful contributions, having shown, under certain simplifying hypotheses:

- that if the actors are left to operate freely, that is to say in the absence of State intervention, the economy converges towards an equilibrium of supply and demand in the case of all goods and services, each having a well defined price.

- that this equilibrium is Pareto optimal, that is to say that in moving away from it, one cannot increase utility for one person without diminishing it for someone else.

2. The Austrian School. this school employs methodological individualism, that is to say it starts with the motivation and behavior of individuals in order to explain collective economic phenomena. Thus it explains the behavior of the firm by the motivations of its personnel, while the State is explained by the motivations of those in power. Austrian economics claims to be a branch of the general theory of human action, also known as "praxeology". Its name arises because its principal contributors were Austrians. Among them the best known are Ludwig von Mises and Friedrich von Hayek but Jean-Baptiste Say and Frederic Bastiat are

universally regarded as precursors of the school.

The Austrians level several criticisms at the neo-Classicists. First is their limiting their gaze to the optimization of existing resources, when in reality the "Entrepreneur"[3] never ceases creating new resources which swiftly render the hypotheses of the neo-Classicist models obsolete. The pie is not fixed, but ever expanding. In the same vein they see the idea of an equilibrium economy as static, even if that equilibrium is attained by a process of convergence, while the real economy is dynamic: the equilibrium of the neo-Classicists will never be achieved, since entrepreneurs constantly exploit disequilibria to create new products and services. For the same reason, neo-Classicists cannot make reliable forecasts.

This does not mean that all the neo-Classical conclusions are false, or interest in this school would have vanished long ago. But some of their conclusions are also reached by the Austrians through a different approach, and the others remain uncertain because of the lack of realism in the hypotheses from which they are derived.

In addition, the following reproach is made to some neo-Classical economists (few in number, it is true): since they think they have a sound grasp of the conditions of equilibrium, they believe that there is nothing to stop the State from calculating these conditions (especially since the advent of large computers) and imposing them in such a way as to accelerate convergence towards equilibrium. Thus they supply a justification for State intervention in the economy.

3. The Keynesian School. Besides John Maynard Keynes, one finds among his followers the American Nobel Prize Laureate James Tobin (celebrated in France by ATTAC for the wrong reasons).[4] The Keynesian methodology is close to that of the neo-Classical's (some use made of the scientific method and models) but is radically different from it in two ways:

- It works on measurable aggregates. This is what is known as "macro economics".

---

3 For the meaning of this word, see chapter 16 and especially note 2.
4 See *ATTAC ou l'intoxication des personnes de bonne volunte*. Jacques de Guenin. Editions, Charles Coquelin. Paris. 2004.

- It regards the State, a priori, as one of the agents of the economy and recommends the measures that should be used for regulating it.

The Keynesian School's success arises from its having seemingly permitted the resolution of recurring economic crises by State intervention. Keynes recommended an increase in public expenditure and a reduction in taxes during times of recession, even if it produces government deficits. At a time of inflation, on the contrary, there should be balanced budgets and an increase in taxes, to pay down the deficits, and even create a surplus, in order to save up for the next cycle. Needless to say that all the world's governments have rushed to adopt these recommendations in periods of recession, at least as concerns public expenditure. However, these same States have proved politically incapable of reducing their expenditures in time of inflation. The success of Keynesian management turned out to be ephemeral - all the more so because Milton Friedman had in the meantime shown that the main cause of economic crises was incompetent management of money by the government.

The fact remains that a theory which justifies the intervention of the State in the economy cannot fail to please the ruling class which controls the government, and people will not be surprised to learn that this approach is still taught at the French Ecole Nationale d'Administration, which educates the elite of the civil service, virtually to the exclusion of all the others.

4. The Marxist School. There are no longer notable economists who identify with it, such have been the catastrophes it has produced in the Communist societies. We still find numerous vestiges of it, however, notably in French (and American) universities.

Its method is very largely ideological, even if Karl Marx used a bit of algebra in Capital to give it a scientific look. In practice it rests on the class struggle and the idea that the "workers" are exploited by the owners of capital.

It is not necessarily Marx's analyses which were false, but the conclusions he drew from them for ideological purposes. Marx and Bastiat, who were contemporaries, both saw the importance of capital accumulation and the tendency of some men to exploit others. They did not, however, draw the same conclusions from this. Marx predicted a growing pauperization of the masses in the capitalist countries. Bastiat thought that a capitalism which respected individual rights would engender unprecedented prosperity in all social classes and the development of a progressively larger middle class. This is exactly what happened in capitalists societies which respect individual freedoms.

Marx predicted that the profitability of capital was fated to decline and that the struggle for new markets would entail wars, and in the long run, the destruction of capitalism, which it would be a good idea therefore to speed up. Bastiat thought that true free exchange between the nations would bit-by-bit eliminate the risk of war, a claim of which the European Union has given a striking confirmation.

For moral reasons which we have amply developed in Part Two, liberals are opposed to the intervention of the State in the economy. Liberal economists are to be found, therefore, only in the ranks of the neo-Classicals and Austrians. The great majority of neo-Classical scholars are, indeed, liberal, but not all of them. Some accept a moderate State intervention. On the other hand, all the Austrians are liberals.

It still remains to be shown that the liberal economy is not only the most moral but also the most efficient. This is what we will illustrate in the following chapters. One should not be astonished by this. The progress in living standards and in people's feelings of mutual solidarity results from the behavior of individuals and the millions of interactions they have with each other. It is the duty of the State to ensure that these interactions take place in full freedom, without violence or destruction. The State must not suppress the free market.. Once a Civil Servant intervenes in these interactions, other than to ensure the complete absence of coercion, he complicates them, delays them, makes them more costly, sometimes to the point of discouraging them.

The Internet gives us a striking demonstration of the superiority of laissez-faire to interventionism. This is a marvelous tool of communication and knowledge, within the reach of all at an increasingly lower price-per-head. It has developed in complete freedom. Who could imagine for a second that the Internet would have been such a massive developmental success, if it had been conceived and controlled by one or more states?

Chapter 15. Free Exchange, the Market and Prices

The market reveals priorities, informing firms what they have to do to satisfy the public best. Competition obliges firms to follow these signs and to adapt.

Jacques Garello[1]

Exchange is the simplest economic act. The individual obtains access thereby to goods and services he cannot or does not wish to make himself. The most common forms of exchange are purchase, sale and letting or renting out of goods and services. This means in turn that one of the goods exchanged is almost always money. The sum of money exchanged for a good is the price of that good. The sum given each month in exchange for delivery of a service is called "earnings". It is the price of labor that the producer (here the worker) charges the consumer (here the employer, his boss) for his time.

As we saw in Part Two, exchange is a natural right. Any person who has made or honestly acquired a product, must be able to exchange it with whomever he likes world-wide, at a price on which the two parties agree. To deprive him of this right to satisfy the convenience of a lobby, is to legitimate theft.

When exchange is free, the satisfaction of both parties is greater afterwards than before, or they would not do it. If one party is adversely affected, this is perhaps because the other has lied to him, but most commonly because the exchange is not totally free - for example because it is subject to regulations imposed by the State. It is also perhaps because the trade is done with a monopoly, that is to say an entity with exclusive powers conferred on it by the State, for no monopoly can maintain itself indefinitely without the State's armed support. This is why economic liberalism recommends non-intervention by the State in production and exchange, outside the protection it owes to individuals to protect them against fraud and theft.

---

1   *Balance of Trade. In Economic Sophisms,* 1845.

The possibility of trading with numerous people is facilitated by the existence of "markets", places (or processes) where people who sell and those who buy can meet (or communicate). There is scarcely a context in the world where people are freer in their decisions than in a market. Certain Marxist "economists" have a lot to say about the "dictatorship of the market", but strictly speaking the coupling of these two words is devoid of meaning.

When there are a number of buyers and sellers for a particular good in a market, a single price for this good is set rather quickly. This is called the equilibrium price, because at this price the demand for and supply of the good are in balance or equilibrium. This equilibrium, however, is fragile: if the number of such goods on the market declines and the demand for them remaining the same, the price will rise. This constitutes a signal for potential sellers, who will be attracted by this new price and will enter the market with additional goods. In the opposite case, if a producer finds some way of making the good at a lower price than the market price at present, he will make greater profits and will put more on the market and the price of the good will fall. If it falls below the production costs of another supplier, the latter will cease production, and the quantity of goods will drop.

The good or service in question may be a constituent of some more complex product, made by another manufacturer. This latter will calculate at any point the cost of the final product and will put it on the market only if this cost is less than the market price of the product. In a free economy, this is what is happening at each moment with the millions of negotiations between people's wishes and the costs of achieving them. The intervention of the State in order to fix such and such a price, for example the price of labor or of a medicine, is a disaster pure and simple, because it leads to bad economic decisions.

In fact, whether the issue is unemployment, shortage of accommodation, shortages of nurses or surgeons, or the everlasting Social Security deficit, there are no great problems of society that the free market cannot handle. On the contrary, each and every attempt to fix them by authoritarian means simply replaces former shortcomings by new ones. In France, this is sadly witnessed by what is now the 21st reform of Social Security at the moment of these words being written.

The disaster is total when the State fixes all prices and quantities in an arbitrary way, as was the case in the Communist countries of sinister memory. Information on society's true needs, routinely born by market prices, is lacking, and production decisions can no longer be taken save arbitrarily. It was while working on this kind of analysis that the great Austrian economist, Ludwig von Mises, had predicted the inevitable failure of the Communist economies.

Only exchanges by persons, physical or moral, (associations or firms) are substantively real. Commercial exchanges between nations have no concrete basis. They are only the totted up aggregations of trading between individuals or companies. This is why economic Liberalism employs methodological individualism in its reasoning. There are economic doctrines which reason on the basis of aggregate phenomena, as we have just seen in Chapter 14. All well and good to them, but this approach is not without danger. Many governments attach a great importance to the trade balance of their countries and are delighted when exports exceed imports. Now such thinking constitutes a sophism, as Bastiat demonstrated abundantly more than 150 years ago. In a famous apologue1, he explains that a businessman exported 200,000 francs worth of French products to the United States. This sum he converted into cotton, shipped this to France, paid the customs due, and brought back 422,000 francs to Bordeaux, which, all payments deducted, left him 85,000 francs to the good. This trade is obviously good for him, a Frenchman. Since France has imported more than she exported, however, her balance of trade was therefore unfavorable in the classical sense. Let us look therefore at an example of a very favorable balance says Bastiat sarcastically. "I dispatch the same cargo to the United States, but a storm sinks the boat. The Customs records show an export, which has improved the balance of trade." He ends by noting that storms being unpredictable, the government should use a more reliable method and throw into the sea all the merchandise leaving the port.

Public opinion, which States ill-inform, holds that exports favor national employment and imports work to its detriment. Hence arises the tendency to protectionism earlier mentioned in Chapter 6. Despite the indefatigable efforts by Bastiat and all the economists worth the name after him to strangle this sophism, it maintains itself in good trim. This explains how public opinion is mobilized by conservative unions against Chinese imports. Until recently China was in an abyss of destitution and poverty caused by Communism. Today, with the liberalizing of the economy she is undergoing an explosion of prosperity. The earnings of Chinese workers have not, however, caught up yet with ours. Products which demand a lot of labor-power are therefore cheaper to manufacture there than in the West and the freeing of trade with China entails an increase in imports for us. Let us examine, therefore, what the consequences of this are.

When a poor French mother buys a Chinese-made blouse for her daughter for €25, of the sort she paid €45 for previously, she saves €20. With these €20 she can give her family red meat three times for dinner. With the €25 the Chinese producer can buy beauty products in France for resale in China. What is the overall balance sheet? Globally French economic activity has lost nothing. Textiles are down €45 but food has gained €20 and perfumery €25. The great gainer is the poor mother, who now has both her blouse and her steaks.[2]

Of course we know right away what the reaction of the protectionists will be. If the textile industry loses outlets, it will have to shed labor. True, but in compensation, the food and perfume industries will increase theirs. If we want employees made redundant by competition to find other jobs easily, we need to support greater fluidity in the labor-market. This is what happens in certain countries like Britain and New Zealand, although they have somewhat socialist governments, or even in Hong Kong, which is a region within a Communist State. In these countries unemployment is very low or does not exist. In France, on the contrary, everything is done to put a brake on the adaptation process, and the results are manifest in unemployment. We will come back to this in Chapter 17.

Let us take another example. Cotton planters in the United States get half their income from Federal Government subsidies. This helps them to live well but at the cost of producing a surplus which contributes to the collapse of world prices. Meanwhile Africa - which produces the most competitive cotton in the world, and needs so much to sell it in order to acquire infra-structure - finds itself cut out of the market by competitors subsidized by the richest State on earth.

Things are no better in Europe. Let us take the example of sugar when the world price was €212 per ton. The price guarantee within the European

---

2   Of course, with his €25, the Chinese producer can buy products from another Eurozone country but he minimizes the freight costs if he buys in France.

Union was €632 - in other words three and a half times higher. European producers profit from these subsidies to reduce their surpluses and they contribute thereby to slashing prices. Hence the succinct conclusion made by that subtle connoisseur of the poverty in the world, Yves Montenay: "The State is a small group of people who contrive to have sugar paid three times its real price, thereby impoverishing the citizens they are supposed to protect, denying foreign peasants access to a better life, and all this so that a friendly clique of the said State can fill its pockets."

When, by contrast, rich countries accept free trade, poor countries benefit immediately. Until quite recently, Holland subsidized its growing of flowers heavily and Uganda, despite its much lower labor costs, could compete only in winter. Since Holland removed these subsidies, however, in eleven years Ugandan exports have increased from near zero to €16m. The children of the peasants who grow these flowers eat better and can now go to school. If free trade becomes general, they will probably come to Europe as tourists one day.

In transition periods, when restrictions on the movement of goods are suddenly removed, competition between firms in different countries can be exacerbated by the differences in the levels of pay from one country to another. It is important to note, however, that over the years, free trade reduces disparities in the average living standards between different nations. To convince oneself of this, all that is needed is to imagine that there had always been free movement of people, goods and capital. It is clear that living standards would have been more or less the same in the different countries of the world. An empirical confirmation of this is given by the evolution of living standards in Japan, a country which once closed itself to the world and where protectionism was extreme, but today is open to free trade. After WWII, Japanese earnings were a fraction of the West's, and we were afraid of that country's competition. Today the Japanese come as tourists to spend their money in our best hotels.

To sum up, let us note that the abolition of economic barriers is always beneficial to the consumer. It hurts certain producers but benefits others. Overall, it raises living standards. The transitions, however, can be difficult for certain categories of workers. So the State, the national education system, businesses and unions, rather than clinging to the existing protectionist arrangements, ought to do everything to facilitate these transitions.

Chapter 16. Business, Competition and Monopoly

Public administration and private activity both have our good in view. But their services differ in that we suffer the former under compulsion, and accept the latter of our own free will; whence it follows that it is reasonable to entrust the former only with what the latter is absolutely unable to carry out.

Frederic Bastiat[1]

The firm is an entity which produces goods and services which customers like sufficiently for them to buy with their own money. This is a key difference with respect to services provided by the State, which are forced on us, be they good or bad, and which we pay for with money taken from us by coercion.

There are only just two kinds of firms: those which are subject to competition and those which are in a monopoly situation. A firm subject to competition is obliged to sell its products at not much more than their cost and to keep their costs at the lowest possible level. It is therefore endlessly constrained to be efficient. A monopoly does not have this problem. It is possible that the manager of a government-owned industry protected by a monopoly, for example, the SNCF, the French Railway System (or Amtrak, the US government's national passenger equivalent), might seek, like his counterpart in a private firm, to produce at the least possible cost. To do this, however, as Henri Lepage explains in The New Industrial Economy (La Nouvelle Economie Industrielle), he is obliged to seek information from his departments whose expenditures he is supposed to control. However, the bureaucrat who works in his government office always has an interest in producing more expensively: better equipment, lighter work-loads, more secretaries, tolerated absences, official vehicles, better retirement benefits, union pressure, etc.

Private business suffers from the same tendencies. Each department tries to extract the maximum it can get from the general management. In this case, however, there is a counterforce, competition, which makes

---

1   Profession of Faith "To the Electors of the Arrondissement of Saint Sever". 1946.

imperative the search for data on competitors. If they have lower prices, then the firm must do better, or it will be pushed out of the marketplace.

A monopoly can exist on a long term basis only if it is imposed by the State, either by regulations or by its being bestowed with legally-protected price advantages making competition virtually impossible, as in the case of a government-controlled national education system.[2] A private monopoly cannot last long. When a firm discovers a new product, or a form of management making it superior to competitors, it will find itself de facto in a monopoly situation which will encourage it to raise its prices. The gains it makes, however, will on the one hand lure it into a certain laxity and on the other attract some envious glances. Sooner or later, some entrepreneur[3] will establish himself in this niche and create competition. For every IBM, there is an Apple Computer waiting to take over the market.

As for the famous "collusions" between firms, intended to reduce competition and maintain remunerative prices, they never last very long either: at the agreed price between competitors, one of them will find it profitable to increase its share of the market – or perhaps a third outfit will set itself up in the market – by offering a lower price. The oil cartel OPEC is noted for rampant cheating by its members. This is why the legislative arsenal against monopolies and agreements is a waste of time - it consumes needed resources and wastes the time of businesses which have better things to do than defend themselves against pointless legal proceedings. This ultimately increases their pass-along costs to their customers. There is no other advantage save to permit politicians to get the people to believe they are defending their interest. Since some businessmen themselves wish to support certain ententes at certain times, for example for nationalistic purposes, the legislation is vague and full of snares for the businessman. When the entrepreneur is hounded to enter into restrictive agreements, he never knows beforehand on what grounds judges will base their pursuit of him in court. Often what is involved is a parody of justice. And the

---

2   In the case of State schools, however, the quality of the product has so far deteriorated since WWII, that certain parents have been led to create private schools, effectively paying twice for their children's education.

3   In the language of economics, an "entrepreneur" is someone who starts things up. This is a more or less a mythical figure, who represents the head of the firm, his advisers and immediate collaborators. To move this entourage in the direction of common objectives, in truth one needs a person of character, endowed with initiative, hence that personalisation.

consumers are fooled into thinking that the State is protecting them.

In a free market, a firm can survive only as long as it satisfies its customers and employees and creates more wealth than it consumes. If a competitor appears who satisfies the customers more because its products are better or cheaper, then the firm must either adapt or perish. If the tastes and needs of the customers change, and they change often, then it is equally imperative that the firm adapt or die. The key word is "adaptation". Unfortunately, in France, the education system, the unions, local and central government - all of them - fret about maintaining existing arrangements rather than helping the firms adapt to new circumstances.

The Marxists spread the idea about the power of the big corporations, with the claim that some have a turnover greater than the Gross National Product of small States. This is a sophism. When, in the 1980s the Japanese succeeded in making cheaper and better cars, General Motors, then the world's largest corporation, and PSA, one of the largest car manufacturers in Europe, almost collapsed. They survived only by themselves taking up the particularly inventive Japanese-style methods of industrial organization. IBM, once thought invulnerable, almost sank in the face of competition from portable computers. More than three hundred thousand businesses go bankrupt every year in the Western world, thirty to fifty thousand of them in France. Every year various business magazines give the performance listings of the world's largest businesses. The ranking changes greatly in the course of time. It is not unusual to see prosperous concerns disappear from this ranking in just a few years.

The entrepreneur is the person who observes the society around him, detects new needs to be satisfied and puts into motion the necessary means to achieve this. He is a creative soul who spreads wealth and enables a number of people less gifted or willing to take risks than he to live. He is by far the most useful person in society and people ought to express their admiration for him - which they probably would if he were not denigrated by false economic theories and envied by the less creative politicians who largely dominate opinion-forming. It is not surprising, therefore, that the entrepreneur is virtually absent from literature, the cinema and the theatre, except in grossly caricatured form. There are happy exceptions in the novels of Jules Verne and those of Ayn Rand. In Rand's Atlas Shrugged a totalitarian system insinuates itself bit-by-bit into the American body politic. The hero, Hank Rearden, a self-made man, is brought to trial because he will not voluntarily accede to the demands of government. As is the way with totalitarian regimes, the system seeks to arrange things in such fashion that Rearden will accuse himself publicly in exchange for his freedom. Rearden, however, is made of sterner stuff. Here is what he says to his judges:

"...I work only for my own profit – which I make by selling a product they need to people who want to buy it and have the necessary means. I make nothing for their advantage to the detriment of my own. They buy nothing to my advantage to the detriment of theirs. I do not sacrifice my interests to them, nor they theirs to me. We deal as equals, by mutual consent to mutual advantage and I am proud of every cent I have earned in this way. I am rich and I am proud of every cent I possess. I have earned my money by my own efforts, in free exchange and with the free agreement of all those with whom I have dealings, the free agreement of those who employed me when I was starting out, the free agreement of those who work for me today and the free agreement of those who buy my product.

I will reply to all the questions you are scared to ask me openly. Do I want to pay my workers more than their services are worth to me? No, I do not. Do I want to sell my product for less than my clients are willing to pay? No, I do not. Do I want to sell it at a loss or give it away? No. If that is bad, do what you will with me, according to your own standards. Here are mine: I earn my own living, as every honest man must. I refuse to feel guilty for my life and the fact that I must work to sustain it. I refuse to feel guilty about being able to do it and do it well. I refuse to feel guilty about the fact that I do it better than most people, of the fact that my work is more valuable than that of my neighbors and that more people want to pay me for it. I refuse to apologize for my abilities and I refuse to apologize for my success. I refuse to apologize for my money."

Let's be fair. There exist, or have existed throughout history, intelligent socialists who understand perfectly well the exceptional qualities which entrepreneurs must have to survive. Take, for example, what Jean Jaurès wrote in the Toulouse newspaper La Dépêche on the 28th May, 1890:

"Members of the capitalist class are invariably courageous. At all times the capitalist class establishes itself by its courage and its conscious acceptance of risk. The capitalist is the man who risks what others do not wish to risk. The man who gains respect is he who accomplishes for others, difficult or

dangerous acts. The boss is he who provides security for others by taking risk onto his own head. Courage for the entrepreneur is the spirit of business and the refusal to go running to the State. For the engineer, courage is the refusal to budge on questions of quality. For the Director of Personnel or the Works Director, it is the defense of authority with respect to the Firm, the House Brand, and within the Firm the maintenance of discipline and order. In the average firm there are many bosses who double as their own cashiers, their own accountants, their own draughtsman, their own foremen, and they have, along with physical tiredness, mental anxieties that the workers know only intermittently. They live in a world of struggle where fellow-feeling is unknown and have no certain shelter against a bankruptcy which can in a day destroy an industrialist's wealth and credit. There is merciless struggle between producers, and in their fighting for customers in years of crisis, they lower the market price of goods to the very limit. They even sell at times below the market price and are obliged to allow enormous delays in payments due, which for those who buy from them create a margin which may lead to their own bankruptcy. Finally, if they suffer the least reverse, the ever watchful banks want to be paid in 24 hours. When the workmen accuse the bosses of being pleasure-seekers who want to make a lot of money just to amuse themselves, they do not understand the bourgeois spirit. Doubtless there are bosses who enjoy themselves but when they are real bosses, what they want above all is to win the battle. Many of them, building up their fortune, will allow themselves no other pleasure. In any event, it is not about that they dream. They are happy, faced with a good inventory, to reflect that all that care and devotion is not wasted, that there is a positive, palpable result, that something came of all the risks, and that their power to get things done has increased. No, in truth, being a boss, in the way that society has shaped this condition, is not an enviable one. Men should not regard one another with feelings of anger or envy. Rather they should practice a kind of reciprocal pity which might even be a prelude to justice itself".[4]

---

4   Quoted by Maurice Levy, director of the Cercle Libéral de Strasbourg, on the site des "Cercles Libéraux".

Chapter 17. Unemployment and Full Employment

*Between unemployment and the calling into question of our in-
stitutional rigidities, we have preferred unemployment: the insecurity
of some was the price to pay for the security of others: the price, higher
and higher down the years, the invoice of our rigidities.*

Alain Madelin[1]

Full employment is the most important objective which a government
can espouse:

- first, because unemployment is contrary to personal dignity.
Dignity demands that one should not be a charge on others, such that one
should produce as much wealth as one consumes in order to live.

- second, because assistance to the unemployed entails obligatory
levies on those in work, and as we shall see, these levies themselves
contribute to aggravating the unemployment. They create, that is to say, a
vicious circle.

- above all, however, because when there is full employment,
negotiations between employer and employee favors the worker. A
significant source of social tension is thereby eliminated.

The paradox is that the only way for a government to achieve full
employment is for it to disengage altogether from the labor market, to
leave employers and employees to contract freely between themselves, and,
more generally, not to intervene in the economy. This is what we propose
to demonstrate in this chapter.

For more than twenty years France has experienced a rate of
unemployment in the region of 10%, whatever the political complexions
of successive governments. Everyone believed that you could increase
employment by means of new administrative methods, by subsidizing at
great cost jobs for which there was no demand at the market price, or by
creating pointless "make work" jobs in the public sector. These measures

---

1   *Chers compatriotes*, Jean-Claude Lattès, 1994.

have all had the effect, direct or indirect, of increasing the cost and complexity of employment. "We have tried everything," as a President of the Republic has been heard to say. Well, France has not tried the one measure capable of generating full employment: the disengagement of the State from economic activity. (In the US, the real U6 unemployment rate is around 18% while bailouts, "stimulus" and "quantitative easing" programs by Washington have dumped over 2 trillion dollars of funny-money on the problem - with little success).

To understand what follows properly, we must first of all refute three sophisms which prevent most people from reflecting adequately on these questions.

1. The false view that there are clear limits to the absorbable output of an economy.

Contrary to what Malthusians believe (they are numerous in France disguised as "greens"), there is no practical limit to the quantity of goods and services that a country like France can absorb. The people who think the contrary have not pushed hard enough with their thinking on two other of their preoccupations: the reduction of poverty which still exists in France and the general increase in living standards. To reduce poverty means to make available more goods and services for the poorest group than they have at present, and therefore to increase production. To raise living standards means to make available to the whole population more goods and services than they have today. In both cases it means producing more and therefore working more. In this perspective, the arbitrary establishment under French law of the 35 hour maximum work week has necessarily been a major economic absurdity.

2. The false view that State legislation should accompany rising productivity by reducing the individual's working time.

Is it not right that the State should go along with technical progress – which permits more output with fewer people – by progressively lowering the legal limit of work? The answer is no. In a perfectly free economy, each person would calculate the trade-offs between his or her standard of living and the time he or she spends working. Individuals would choose that equilibrium level of activity allowing the closest approximation to their wishes. Full employment permits firms to offer much greater variation in hours worked than is permitted by today's legislation, in order to recruit people they need, since - let us say it again - under full employment firms compete with one another to satisfy their labor needs, contrary to what happens today. This variation makes it much easier for mothers to find jobs which allow them more free time to be with their children in return for less pay. And conversely it allows for young fathers to work longer for more money to raise the family's standard of living.

3. The false claim that the State can create new jobs.

All money spent by the State to create jobs destroys jobs - somewhere else and in larger numbers. Let us suppose the State spends €100 to "create" a job, directly or by way of subsidy. This is what is visible to the observer. As Bastiat explains, however, in What is Seen and What is not Seen, this €100 does not fall from heaven. It is going to be taken by way of taxation from someone else's income. This revenue-raising itself has a cost (say, €10), so the income of this other person will be cut by €110. If this money had been left with him, he could have bought something useful for himself with it, say, a jacket. Now he cannot and the jacket-maker - who now sells one less jacket - will have to cut his labor-force. The "creation" of a job by the State, thus destroys more than one job elsewhere. This is what is not seen - by the press, the politicians, or the public. This works when the job "created" is useful. It fails, however, when the State "creates" a "make-work" job. Then one useful job, which served to produce goods and services sufficiently appreciated for people to buy them, is destroyed. This is how living standards are lowered.

The liberation of the labor market signals would entail the end of labor legislation and the establishment of specific contracts, freely negotiated between employer and employee, helped (or not) by his Union. The role of the State could be limiting itself to supplying simplified contracts to help the numerous illiterates formed in the bosom of the State schools.. All sorts of contracts now buried might thus see the light of day, much more adapted to the reciprocal needs of individuals and firms than any legislation could conceive.

Such liberation would include the abolition of the minimum wage. The existence of a minimum wage in fact prevents hundreds of thousands of people from gaining work. Let us supply two examples:

Miss Durand, an elderly, retired teacher, who gets around only with difficulty and can no longer see well, needs a female companion to keep her company, do the shopping and the housework. She could feed her, lodge her and pay her €500 a month, the most she could afford from her pension. Mr. and Mrs. Dupont have a daughter, Juliette, a bit asthenic, a little retarded, but lively and a happy soul, unemployable at the level of the official government-mandated SMIC (Salaire Minimum Interprofessionnel de Croissance) the index-linked, guaranteed minimum wage of €1424 per month before tax. Without this minimum wage law, Miss Durand is free to hire Juliette. The parents are delighted and so is Juliette. She is going to be able to make herself useful and accumulate some small savings... until the visit of the "Social Worker", a civil servant called in to enforce the official pay arrangements. This lady hits the ceiling. Juliette cannot be paid less than what is laid down by the SMIC. Alas, it is impossible for Miss Durant to pay her at the SMIC level; the magnificent arrangement is in ruins. Everybody is distressed. Miss Durand will have to go to a retirement home. Juliette will receive unemployment benefit which will diminish over time.

Christopher, holder of a CAP ("certificat d'aptitude professionnelle" or vocational training certificate) as a motor mechanic, is trying to get a job at an automobile garage. He feels he is wasting his time at his Technical High School. He is also ashamed to be dependent on his parents who themselves have difficulty making ends meet. Michael, owner of a local garage, is swamped with work. He would like to hire another employee, - someone already experienced- for he doesn't have the time to train a novice. Moreover, a beginner doesn't know enough to do expensive work which will pay for Michael to cover the statutory minimum wage he would have to pay a beginner.

Christopher, however, wants to work and approaches Michael, saying: "Start me at €450 a month. I will do enough for you to justify this modest wage. I will learn by watching and imitating you. You can pay me more to the extent that I make progress."

"What you say is right enough," says Michael, "but absolutely illegal. If something happened to you, I would be hard put to avoid ruin."

"All right. Let me give you a written request for a voluntary placement. We can renew it every month and you can pay me on the side. In case of accident, I will assume the responsibility. My parents will come to you to confirm it".

"I know your parents. They are reliable people. I think I can put my faith in them. I know I am taking a big risk, but I like the look of you and I want to give you a break".

At the end of six months, our garage owner was so pleased with Christopher that he took him on at the legal minimum wage. Christopher very quickly became much sought after in the market for car mechanics, which did not escape his boss's notice, and the latter gave him regular increases to retain him.

What is clear in this example is that no one will ever be employed unless his or her marginal cost (earnings plus social security costs etc.) is lower than the marginal revenue which this worker brings to the enterprise. Now, under minimum wage laws, the actual level of the combination of minimum pay plus social security charges precludes the employment of many people whose revenue to the firm would be less than they cost. This includes young people with no qualifications and people who are either less physically robust or more mentally handicapped. If there were freedom of employment and earnings, all these people would be hired for pay which, while certainly below the present national minimum, would nevertheless increase with experience and qualifications. Everyone, moreover, would benefit: the individuals involved, their families, and society itself. Furthermore, we would rapidly reach full employment and at the same time the workers would flourish in their occupations.

To flourish in one's work is:
- to understand the whys and wherefores of what one is doing
- to be able to exercise initiative and responsibility up to the
   level of one's capacities
- to be treated with consideration

Consideration depends on the attitude of one's boss, not on laws and regulations. In the completely rigid system of employment with which we are familiar, where the worker is trapped in the firm, and the boss stuck with the employee he has taken on, the boss has little incentive to go to a lot of trouble looking after his workers. By contrast, in a free labor market, enjoying full employment, a virtuous circle occurs: the boss has to make a great effort to keep the best and the weaker ones have every incentive to try to improve.

Let's not be naïve. We won't find every day of the week, politicians brave enough to bring in free work contracts nor unions clear minded enough to accept them. In the meantime other measures could be put into operation to reduce unemployment. We can spell out the main ones.

The first way of increasing employment is to decrease state expenditure.

We can, first of all, eliminate all the jobs unnecessarily imposed on us by the State. The list is a very long one. We can convince ourselves about this by taking at random any subject whatsoever with which the State busies itself, and by examining the list of the various bodies which concurrently busy themselves with it. Let us take as an example the French Government's "Policy for Towns and Cities".

Below are some of the organizations responsible for this:

- The Inter-ministerial Group with respect to Towns and Cities
  and the Urban Environment
- The National Council of Towns and Cities
- Federation of Bureaus of Urban Development
- Group for Urban Research, Trade and Communication
- Urban Planning
- Regional Land Development Agency
- Ile de France Institute of Urban Planning
- Ministry of Supply, Urban Technical Services
- Centre for the Study of Urbanism
- Urban Studies Branch of the Ministry of Supply
- Fund for Urban Social Action
- Institute for the City
- Various subsidized associations

Since this policy-making has served no purpose in the difficult urban areas, we must necessarily conclude that it's real function is to create "jobs for the boys". The "Ministry for the City", created by President Mitterrand, had no end but to give his political crony Bernard Tapie a portfolio.

This is what the French Audit Office says about this policy:

"It has been marked till now by the imprecision of its objectives and its strategy, and by a liking for publicity which leads it to launch periodically into new measures. The result of this is a host of procedures and a tangled mass of areas of intervention which are difficult to discern".

A current sophism consists in saying: "Yes, but at least these goings-on generate some work". The jobs created this way are what is seen. What is not seen, however, are the jobs destroyed somewhere else, a point we explained earlier. The creation by the State of jobs for which there is no demand, results therefore purely and simply in the destruction of work elsewhere. One can extend this reasoning to all State expenditures having no connection with need.

The next move is to abolish all monopolies.

We showed in the previous chapter how an enterprise enjoying a monopoly inevitably produces goods which cost more than they would be with competition. Thus any good bought for 100 € from a State monopoly, directly, as with EDF ("Electricité de France" - the French national electricity company) or indirectly through taxation, as with mandatory State education, will cost 100 €-x if it is supplied by organizations subject to competition. With x €, the customer would be able to buy extra goods, simultaneously increasing thereby both his living standards and the general level of employment. Foreign comparisons suggest that x equals a few percentage points up to 50%, depending about the public sector concerned.

Once again, let us beware of the sophism: "employment created by x money would merely compensate for the jobs eliminated in a public sector made more efficient" As we saw earlier, any public sector job destroys more than one private job due to the administrative overhead and waste in the government system..

Finally, we could reduce the administrative and fiscal harassment which weighs industry down.

A firm subject to competition constantly improves its performance, and if it is in a "renewal" market (for example electronic devices), it produces every year the same volume of goods with fewer and fewer people. This is perceived negatively because vested interests, unions and local and central government cling to the present situation, rather than favoring adaptation. But, to maintain present arrangements at all costs serves only to diminish living standards, since it is the growth in productivity which lowers prices. At the same time, as our living standards grow, we also have more and more resources available to satisfy our infinite needs. So it is in countries where State supervision is light that new products are created, like computers, cell phones, or flat screen TV's, and small enterprises spring up to deal with new demands, for example the care of children whose mothers go to work.

If we want to resolve the problem of unemployment, we must first of all thoroughly accept the essential truth that it is above all the small firm, existing (or yet to be born) that is most equipped to create employment. Sad to say, France policy and law discourage the rapid growth or creation of firms. For proof, one can ask any workman – painter, plumber etc. – whom you need to hire. If you find one, you will probably have to wait several weeks because he is swamped with work. Ask him why he does not employ a companion. You will be regaled with the most varied responses.

One will tell you that he has tried it already, but that relations with officialdom are much more complicated and irksome once one has an employee. He cannot cope with it. How could one not believe him? The French Work Code has 2,700 pages and the Code for Social Security more than 3,200! Since these Codes increase in size every year, they have long since become unreadable and incoherent. But God help the business manager who doesn't know them! In small businesses the worker would be much better protected by a contract simple enough for him to understand: a contract of twenty pages of commonsense rules. There could be skeleton contracts between which workers and businesses could choose. (Similarly, in the U.S., thousands of pages of rules and regulations are issued by the Federal Government, the States, Counties and Cities - and growing ever larger every year).

Another artisan will tell you he prefers his present scale of operations, but with a well-filled order-book, to a larger scale operation, with the nagging worry about shedding an employee if orders falter.

Another will tell you he is looking for a workmate but has not found one. At the Smic[2] rate, it will cost the business €1424 per month. Now after tax, this worker will earn   net only €930 per month, after the employer turns over to the State the mandatory withholding taxes, fees and other payments. At this rate the employee would prefer to stay at home and live on unemployment benefits. The other way round, when he is an employer, he must pay €1424 to obtain only 152 hours of unqualified labor per month. Therefore, he is very exacting as to the quality and output of the people he initially hires.

The weight of obligatory taxes and fees on earnings is enormous. If one adds the management's share and the workers' share, it oscillates between 60 and 70% of the net salary. This is one of the biggest obstacles to employment. Social Security takes 80% of these levies, of which the largest item is for mandatory sickness insurance. Could one reduce this cost? Certainly if one notes that in France Social Security employs one administrator for every two doctors, and that in spite of this we must buy our own additional insurance on top of Social Security Insurance to cover what the latter does not cover. One way forward would be to include in the employee's pay the present taxation for health purposes, allowing them to take such sickness insurance as they choose, subject to this insurance being obligatory.

Moreover, this is only part of the litany you hear when you ask small businessmen in France why they won't hire new workers. There is the whole taxation system to consider, in all the forms that enterprise must bear: taxes on business and the self-employed, taxes on pay, property-taxes, registration-fees, vehicle-taxes, apprenticeship taxes, profit taxes etc.

This complexity, this harassment - there being no other word - this whole tax-structure, the sheer cost of all these funds levied, inevitably depress the creative potential of business, inevitably discourage the artisan who would like to take on a helper and the farmer who would like to hire a field hand.

If there are still people with the nerve to launch new ventures, they surely must be ignorant of these obstacles. Unfortunately, when they discover them, it is often because the State has made them bankrupt.

---

2   Smic: the French minimum legal wage.

The facts, sad to say, fully confirm the foregoing analysis: for years in France, more or less the same number of enterprises fail as are established. In all the countries where unemployment is low, the State intervenes less in the economy, and far more businesses are created than destroyed.

Chapter 18. Investment, Savings, The Stock Exchange and "Relocation"

The profits of yesterday are today's Investments, which are in turn tomorrow's jobs.

Helmut Schmidt[1]

To create an enterprise and develop it, requires the construction or purchase of equipment and facilities, in other words physical investments. To invest, the firm needs capital, which in turn means access to savings. In the case of small firms, this means personal savings or borrowing. A large firm can issue shares. Whoever buys these shares makes a financial investment. Such an investment is attractive because of its liquidity. This is why every day some people buy shares and others sell them on the stock exchange, a very efficient market in which information circulates perfectly and in real time. Here we have a particularly useful activity, criticized only by the enemies of free enterprise, a group disappearing in the civilized countries but still very active in France.

We saw in the last chapter that workers will be taken on only when their marginal cost (earnings plus charges to the employer) are less than the marginal revenue they bring to the firm.

In a free society, wants are infinite, and there can always be found some entrepreneur to take on a workman or other employee so long as the latter allows the firm to make extra revenue at least equal to the costs (earnings plus other costs) of the person taken on. In economic language we say that at equilibrium earnings are equal to marginal work productivity. How in this context, should we interpret investments which improve the productivity of the firm, that is to say those that permit the same output with fewer people? In a full employment economy, these investments do not destroy labor but they transfer it, with the eventual result of improving the living-standards of all. Another immutable economic law shows us, indeed, that the investments achieved by the firm increase the marginal productivity of every worker: if a worker makes ten items per day, the

---

1   Former German Chancellor

addition of a machine may allow him to produce a hundred. Now, as we have already seen, increased living standards can be attained only through an increase in goods and services produced.

Investment is thus the motor of increasing living standards. Now, the reality is that we can invest only on the basis of funds which have been saved. This can be money earned by the firm, or raised from individuals via banks and savings funds. Unfortunately, in France the State discourages savings by taxing it at three levels. First it taxes incomes. Secondly it taxes interest and dividends on income saved and invested. Thirdly it taxes inheritance. (The same is true in the U.S. and other developed countries). If the State did no more than use this confiscated saving for investment purposes, it would be only half bad – the evil resulting from its inefficiency. In fact, however, it mostly spends it on current uses, not for investment.

Let us turn to physical investments in poor countries. They are mistakenly known as relocating. One says "mistakenly", because if a French company constructs a factory abroad, this is not solely to bring back to France goods made elsewhere, it is also, indeed primarily, to increase its outlets. Here too, to wish to prevent such investment is to wish to prevent the most poor people from advancing, in order to conserve the advantages of the affluent.

For to invest in a poor country is:
- to bring indispensable know-how to the development of local resources
- to produce goods and services which do not exist locally, or which are better or cheaper or respond more satisfactorily to a demand than the existing local products
- to create employment
- to help raise living standards

Thus, the governments of these countries, whatever their political regimes, are always pleading for the setting up of foreign factories in their countries. Thus, Multinationals are therefore always welcome when they invest in this or that place: they are not sought for solely by the politicians in power. They are also much in demand by their employees, and loved by their customers. These simple, unanswerable truths reduce to dust the myth of societies out to exploit the lowly.

It is proper to add that if a firm develops a new activity in a country, it will always operate it much more efficiently than the country's government using foreign aid simply because the company is working with its own invested resources. Perhaps, however, the most important contribution made by multinationals to the progress of suffering humanity, is that they permit men and women of different nationalities to work shoulder-to-shoulder, for common objectives useful to the whole society. They contribute thereby to peace in the world. When you have worked in another country, alongside its people, the idea that you might one day have to go to war with them becomes intolerable.

Corporations are reproached for investing in countries where labor is cheaper. Is it not better, however, to offer some employment on the spot to the workers in these countries, than to leave them to emigrate, often under inhuman conditions?

The free circulation of individuals, ideas, goods and capital, engender prosperity, increase economic growth, and in diminishing poverty and inequality are favorable to peaceful relations between nations.

All this is so unarguable, so soundly established by the facts, that one might well wonder why there are still people so hostile with respect to the issue. It is quite simply because the truth inconveniences them and they do not want to know. Such people fall into two categories. In the first we find those who are too attached to their privileges and do not want to make any effort to adapt, because it is too tiresome. Included here are businesses in fear of foreign competition and turned in on themselves, unions and governments. In the second we find all those committed to collectivist or interventionist ideologies. Now all ideology, as is well-known, creates an impenetrable barrier to knowledge of the facts.

Chapter 19. Money

There is very valuable evidence, covered up by official teaching, which bears witness to the effect that everywhere a free banking system has existed, there has been no inflation and no economic cycles, while at the same time countries with central banks enjoying a monopoly of note issue, experienced such crises.

Philippe Nataf[1]

Different goods have proved suitable as a medium of exchange at different times in history. For a good to be acceptable as money, it must have several attributes. It must be valuable and easy to manipulate and must not deteriorate as a result of handling. Copper, then silver, then gold, were the standard metals used as money.

In 1157 the Bank of Venice was born in that city. The people came to deposit their money there, in this instance in gold pieces, and were given receipts in exchange. This was the first deposit bank; there have been a lot of others since. These banks obviated the need to move metallic money. To pay a supplier, a merchant could arrange a transfer from his account to the supplier's. The bank offered this service and made it pay. A natural extension was to issue notes convertible at any moment into money and allowing purchases and settlements without movement of coins. This was a useful innovation, which furthermore (in principle at least) offered security against theft, to the extent that the notes were numbered. Gold was deposited at the bank, which served as a safe or strongbox. If one wished to recover one's gold, it was just a matter of returning the notes to the bank, which reimbursed them in gold.

Before long, the banks began lending. They either lent funds they had, or funds which they borrowed, normally at a rate of interest higher

---

1   This quotation is taken from a lecture delivered by Philippe Nataf to the Cercle Frédéric Bastiat, on December 9th 2000. The whole text is available on the website www.bastiat net, under the section "The Activities of the Cercle Bastiat", The texts of earlier dinner-debates". Some of the data in this chapter are taken from this lecture. Moreover, several paragraphs in this chapter, are taken from my book *ATTAC ou l'intoxication des personnes de bonne volonté, (ATTAC: Or Poisoning People of Good Will)* Institut Charles Coquelin, 2004.

than the one they borrowed at. Insofar as they lent their own or borrowed funds, they did   not create money. Later they began to create money, employing the following means: let us take the case of a merchant who makes a sale worth 1000 francs, payable in three months. He gets from his client a "bill of exchange", an agreement to pay in three months. He deposits this bill of exchange at his bank, which agrees to pay him immediately IOU notes valued at 1000 francs, less a discount of 6%. This means that for three months he loses 1.5%, receiving only 985 francs. Now we have 985 francs which did not exist before but are now in circulation in addition to the previous money supply. Money created like this is called bank money or deposit money.

From the nineteenth century most nations established central banks to which they gave monopoly powers for the issuing of these IOU notes. Until 1914 the central banks of the great western Nation States offered free convertibility of notes into gold, and these notes maintained a stable value, at least when expressed in gold. In the nineteenth century the French franc was worth 282 mg of gold. From 1914 convertibility was abolished and notes afterwards have continued to decline in value.

The dishonest manipulation of money is an instrument currently used by States to spend more than they raise from their subjects in the form of taxation. It had existed earlier when there were kings, the latter on occasion reducing the proportion of gold in the coinage to create themselves some extra resources, though these soon ran out if their majesties continued to spend too much.

If in the course of a year, a government receives 100 and spends 110, it must either borrow the 10 or issue money which is not backed by any financial asset. The first option cannot go on indefinitely. If it goes on year after year the State's indebtedness must necessarily increase. At the same time its lenders will demand higher and higher rates of interest, and increasingly substantial guarantees, until the point when they get tired and will no longer lend. At this point recourse to the second method becomes necessary. The money is devalued. Its purchasing power diminishes. There is inflation.

The stability of a currency is all the more precious if one is uneducated or badly off: educated people find ways of protecting themselves against inflation and even of benefiting from it. Less well off people who painfully put a bit of money aside each month to pay for consumer durables, see their savings eroded by the fall in the value of money. Viewed in this light, Inflation is theft.

There are 174 central banks in the world. The great majority of them which are subject to the governments in power in their countries are a complete disaster. Some thirty only are reasonably managed (which is to say subject to low inflation for a few years in a row). As many as sixty one developing countries have experienced an average rate of annual inflation greater than 10% for the last ten years.

In money matters liberals generally agree on one point: money is much too important to be entrusted to Nation States. They differ only on the practicalities of managing money by non-state means. These differences, however, relate more to the perception of what is realistic in a given context, than to a disagreement over the relative desirability of different policy options. The first step is to entrust the management of money to an institution independent of any government, and whose sole objective is to maintain the value of that money. This is the case with the European Central Bank, and partly true of the American Federal Reserve (though this latter Bank also aims at growth and full employment).

These two institutions, however, are criticized by liberals, as insufficiently independent of government. The State often appoints their Boards of Directors, and can put pressure on them in various ways. So the next stage is to eliminate all possibility of States interfering in money matters. They are then constrained to balance their budgets, at least over several years.

Three types of money management independent of the State have been used in the past. They are described below in growing order of efficiency:

1. Currency Boards which link the local currency, rigidly, with a more stable and more highly regarded international currency, for example the dollar, though the French franc had also been used by France in her colonies. This method can make the local money only as stable as the currency of reference, but it has shown good results in countries undergoing runaway inflation. It was used notably in Argentina between 1991 and 1994.

2. The Gold Standard. This operated between 1795 and 1914 in Western countries. Across this whole period their currencies were not devalued and remained stable. In August 1914 the governments of France, England and Germany decided to abolish currency convertibility. Inflation then appeared, more or less strongly, in these countries. In France, for example, by 1959 the franc had dropped to 5% of its 1914 value. (The U.S. abandoned the gold standard domestically when President Roosevelt confiscated all gold coins from Americans on April 5, 1933; President Nixon unilaterally cancelled the direct convertibility by other Nation States of the United States dollar to gold on August 15, 1971).

However useful the Gold Standard may have been for preventing States from handling money irresponsibly, it is not an absolute guarantee of stability, in the sense that the value of gold in relation to other goods and services, depends on the quantity of gold available. In the sixteenth century, for example, there was a marked inflation in Spain, spreading to the rest of Europe, caused by the huge quantity of gold and silver brought back from Peru by the Spanish Conquistadors.

3. Freedom of money-issue by competing banks. There were areas in the nineteenth century, like Scotland and the six States of New England in the United States, where the private banks were free to issue notes. The extraordinary thing is that there were never any crises in these places. These banks were in fact in competition with each other. If one bank printed too much money in relation to its reserves, its currency depreciated against the other banks. That is to say individuals in a position to determine what was happening, hastened to convert notes issued by that renegade bank into real money provided by the other banks instead. The threat of a bank run forced the bank in question to return very swiftly to a sounder, less exposed policy.

In fact, the habitual inter-bank, call-money payments, drastically limited any impulse towards over-issue.

The Bank of France itself was a free-market bank until 1803, the year when Napoleon, who was one of its main shareholders, granted it a monopoly in the creation of money. Two and a half years later the Bank of France experienced its first crisis: it had issued too much paper, and the people, losing confidence, rushed to change their notes into gold. Coercive measures were needed to prevent their doing so.

Chapter 20. Retirement

The system put in place and bitterly defended by the functionaries and politicians, is there only to serve the functionaries and politicians themselves. As if they had the right to look after themselves without ever having paid anything.

Jean-Jacques Walter[1]

According to the liberal morality we recounted in Part One, we should all assume responsibility for our lives, exercising our individual freedom to live it as we think we should, subject to respecting other people's freedom. To prepare for the time he will no longer be working, the individual owes it to himself, therefore, to save and to employ the money saved in whatever fashion he wishes. In many civilized countries - although not in France - people put it mainly into specialized pension funds which constantly search the best outlets: shares, debentures, real estate, commercial businesses, treasury bonds. On retirement the individual can retrieve his entire capital and re-invest it himself elsewhere, or have it paid to him monthly in the form of a life annuity, or retrieve part of it to be invested in some new activity, leaving the pension fund to continue managing the remainder, etc. Such is freedom. If he dies his beneficiaries will retrieve the remaining capital in the pension fund. The great advantage of this arrangement for society, is that most of the money thus saved is invested, and we saw in Chapter 3.3. that investment in businesses increases employment and augments living standards. This system is called "capitalized retirement".

In France capitalized retirement is not forbidden but the country lacks the institutions to achieve it in a popular and extensive fashion, and the State in any case obliges the French citizen to pay into another system, namely a contributory pension plan (similar to the U.S. Social Security System). Under this last arrangement, each member of the working population pays into one or several accounts : a universal one, called below "the general system", entirely controlled by the State, and some "complementary ones" depending upon the profession of the subscriber. They are controlled by the employers, the unions, and the State . For private sector earnings,

---

1 *Retraite: le désastre annoncé.[Retirement: the predictable disaster]* Edition Sauvegarde Retraites. 2002.

the contribution is deducted from the pay. This contribution gives rise to annuities in the general system and to "points" in the complementary systems. All the money taken by one account is redistributed the same year to the people in retirement who have contributed to this same account at one time in their lives. Where the complementary accounts are concerned, the portion received by each retired person is proportional to the number of points acquired by that person in that account, during the course of his or her career.

Let us remember that under contributory pensions, it is the active population who pay for the retired. This system was imposed after WWII, when millions of prudent people saw their savings vanish, for in a period of high inflation, few people have any way of maintaining the value of their savings by investing them cleverly enough. Hence we saw the introduction of a scheme based on doling out to the retired, money saved the same year by the active population.

To function well, however, the system requires that there be a relatively constant relationship between the numbers of the retired and those of the active population. Now for some years the numbers of those working have decreased (unemployment, falling birth-rate, longer periods of study) while the numbers of retired people grew (lowering of the retirement age, increase in life expectancy). To take an example, when the new dispensation was introduced, the day after WWII ended, a workman retired at 65 and lived on average to 67. Today he retires at 60 and lives on average to 77.

This system by contributory pension is much more complicated in practice than public opinion suspects. According to the work he does, each active soul belongs to a particular category. There are in France no less than 124 special categories – of which, however, 109 are in process of extinction – which include civil and military functionaries, the salaried employees of public enterprise, the personnel of the various Assemblies, of Social Security, of the National Employment Agency, of the social services and state-hospitals, of the Post Office, etc.

This system is also profoundly unjust because of these special categories. The contribution functionaries pay on their salaries, is only 7.85%, whereas the private sector figure is on average 10.35%. The latter, however, will receive a pension only half the size of that of the former. The civil servant's retirement pension is calculated according to the number of years of service on the basis of the salary of the last six months. The fundamental pension of the private sector is based on the twenty five best years. A quarter of the civil servant's pension is financed by his contributions, but three quarters by what he takes from taxpayers' pockets, including taxpayers of the private sector. The pensions of public sector employees, who make up a quarter of the active workforce, cost of the order of €76 billion, against €106 billion for the other 75% who are on private pensions. If the special categories were abolished, the cost of public sector retirement pensions would be only €32 billion.

The elected representatives do better still. Deputies are beneficiaries of a retirement scheme whose payments are a hundred times higher than the contributions they have made.

The French system of retirement by contributory pension schemes is therefore completely immoral. Is it at least better for the average worker than retirement by self-funded pension scheme? It is no such thing.

For a given annual contribution, a self-funded pension scheme is much more advantageous to the worker than a contributory one. This occurs because the worker, at least for that part of his income, finds himself in the same situation as the capitalist. He receives from his investments the same type of income as the capitalist. I have given a simplified but completely worked out example in my book *ATTAC, or the intoxication of people of goodwill*. I have supposed a society where people work for forty years and live for twenty years after retiring. So there are two working citizens for one retired one.

As an example, let's assume that the average pay of a French worker is €1500 per month. Two people at work therefore make €3000 per month.

Contributory System: to finance a retirement income of 60% of one's earnings, say €900 per month, each working person must contribute €450 each month, that is €5,400 per year, some 30% of his earnings.

Self-Funded Scheme: the employee invests the same €5,400 @ 5% per annum. After 40 years he will have accumulated a capital of €652, 320.

He can convert it on the same conditions into a rent for twenty years whose annual payment will be equal to €55, 723, that is €4644 per month.

Thus he will pick up €4644 per month instead of €900. If he reckoned, however, that € 900 would be enough, he could happily contribute €87.2 per month, or 5.85% of his pay, rather than 30%

Of course, to avoid the fluctuations which individual capitalists and companies incur, he must not invest the money intended for his retirement himself, nor invest it in his own company, but make an approach to a specialized firm, a mutual benefit company or insurance company, whose expertise is in the spreading of risks. These societies do not work on a short-term basis, but on the very long-term view, and one of their functions is to smooth out fluctuations. In order to minimize risks in the short and medium terms, they invest part of their funds in real estate, treasury bonds, etc., whose return is less than that of the stock market in the long term but more stable. On average these companies get an annual return of 5.5% on their investments.

Retirement by self-funded pension is at once more moral, simpler, more flexible and more remunerative for the worker. How is it, given these conditions, that private pensions could be so well established in other countries but not in France? It is quite simply because the beneficiaries of the French system, the politicians and functionaries, battle tooth and claw to maintain their privileges. The unions recruit basically in the public sector, and they paralyze the country each time a government tries a timid reform to make the system more equitable to the non-union and non-government workers.

We obviously cannot move without transition from the contributory system to self-funding. Most workers could not both save for their old age while at the same time contribute to existing retirement plans to pay for other people too. It can be done, however, over a long period. This is what Chile managed from 1982 under the leadership of the Minister of Finance, José Pinera. The workers were able in this instance to choose between staying in the contributory system or investing in pension funds. Jose Pinera inspired the creation of fifteen pension funds which both competed and allowed movement between one another. Drastic rules of management were established to guarantee depositors the use of their investments, in accordance with the purpose of a liberal State, which is to guarantee individual rights.[2] The system persuaded more and more Chileans, as soon as they were able to see that their pension funds generated pensions that paid out far more money to them compared with those of the previous State-run plan. Moreover, the additional monies earned in these new pension funds were invested in companies whose expansion has dramatically increased the growth in living standards.

---

2   See Chapter 9.

Chapter 21. Public Choice

The State is not a divine construction endowed with the gifts of ubiquity and infallibility. It is a human organization in which decisions are taken by human beings like any others, neither better nor worse, themselves also liable to make mistakes.

Henri Lepage[1]

One of the great contributions of neo-classical theory was to show that an economy can function very well without a State. Somewhat in reaction to the Keynesians, the Austrian School went further, showing that the State was hardly capable of intervening in the economy without creating catastrophes, these in turn soon "corrected" by new ones. On the basis of methodological individualism, the Austrian School dissected the making of public decisions in order to understand why. The great Bastiat himself was one of the first to have explained this phenomenon, and in his work can be found every one of the concepts described below. Jacques Garello, incidentally, had fun doing precisely this in a brilliant account delivered to the Cercle Bastiat in 1996[2]. In the work of Bastiat, however, these ideas are dispersed and are often subsidiaries of some other subject. The merit of having methodically demonstrated and illustrated all these concepts by linking them to each other under the rubric "theory of public choice" comes from two Americans economists, James Buchanan and Gordon Tullock.

Behind the screen of institutions there are men and women like any others. These people are no better nor worse than any others. They act with regard to their interests in the very broad sense, whether these interests are sordid or edifying. As soon as they have a bit of power, however, they want to increase it - and they abuse it. Lord Acton said: *"All power corrupts and*

---

1   *Demain le capitalisme.* Hachette. Collection Pluriel. 1983.
2   *Décisions publiques et comportement des hommes politiques.* [*Public Decisions and the behavior of politicians.*] The complete text can be found on the website www.bastiat.net, section, "les activités du Cercle Frédéric Bastiat". Texte des precedents diners-débats. Several of the ideas advanced in this chapter are taken from this lecture. In the work of Bastiat, however, these ideas are dispersed and are often subsidiaries of some other subject.

absolute power corrupts absolutely." In exchange for our votes these people promise us "public services", interventions, subsidies, rules and laws. All their craft lies in identifying the hopes and expectations of the various groups of voters and making promises to them.

The wishes of individual voters have no chance of coming to pass unless these individuals   belong to pressure groups. A candidate has no time to listen to one voter. It is much more productive for him to listen to someone who speaks for a group. This explains the power of trade unions. They represent no more than a small minority of voters, but a combination of their privileged status and State largesse allows them to make a lot of noise and nuisance. Thus they can persuade public opinion that they represent a lot of people.

Pressure groups are made up of people with an interest in the State's making fresh expenditures which benefit them - to which the politicians lend themselves very easily. For a pressure group which benefits from public funds, the results are sufficiently rewarding to encourage its members to support a politician who assures it this advantage. On the other hand, the financing of this extra expense will be buried in a mass of taxation and it will not be very visible, nor very much felt, at the level of the taxpaying individual. The phenomenon is contagious, however. People whose personal ethical stance is against advantages obtained at the expense of others, end up asking for other special benefits for themselves or their associations.1 They argue: *"After all, I pay my taxes, so why should I not get some return too?"*

Once elected - but always with an eye to re-election - politicians devote themselves to negotiations with their colleagues to satisfy their voters. Let us imagine a politician who wants to get approved a project favorable to a group of his voters. Another politician may well vote for the project on a tit-for-tat basis, provided it does not offend his own voters, or if he has himself voters who will benefit from this project. "If you will vote for my farmers I will vote for your industrial laborers". Americans call this "log-rolling" on the analogy of the blocks of wood made to roll over one another.

Public expenditure is aggravated by government. The senior bureaucrats are motivated by their importance. Each law will increase that importance by engendering more work and therefore more resources and more personnel.

This analysis helps us understand why public expenditures increase indefinitely. It will never be easy to reverse this phenomenon, in particular because it is very difficult for the voter to form an opinion as to what is truly at stake in a political decision. The media with mass audiences cover mere events, or the superficial opinions of well-known people, or they feed on the quarrels of personalities. They do not supply us with data, or analyses or explanations, or if they do supply a few sensational facts, these are rarely followed by analyses in the slightest bit informative. So, one must devote a lot of time, spend a great deal of energy and collect a lot of information before one can form a clear opinion on any given subject - or on the capacity, or even the sincerity, of this or that politician. One would make this effort if need be, if one thought one's vote could have some influence. This is not, however, the case, because an isolated vote is not effective, as has been seen, if the voter is not part of a pressure group. What good is it then, to go to the trouble of convincing others, when one knows that in any case, whether one is electing a politician of the left or the right, that will change nothing?

The result of the election, in reality, depends on "the median voter". If we classify voters by their thinking along a line, putting at the head of the line those most on the left and on the end of the line those most on the right, the median voter is located at the middle. Around him, in a bipartite system, there is a fringe group of people whose voting intentions one does not know. To win, a candidate must make a special effort with this kind of voter. A candidate who professes a doctrine, who affirms a radical argument, has no chance of being elected. To be elected, one needs a line which pleases without positing anything, one acceptable to the opposition, without displeasing those on one's side. French President Giscard d'Estaing said, "France aspires to be governed at its middle", since it is always in the middle that one looks for the missing votes.

If worst comes to worst, only those voters who think it a duty will vote, or those who may derive specific advantage from doing so. Those who think their vote will count for nothing, prefer to go fishing. This is the attitude which economists of the public choice school call "rational ignorance". When this is what happens, these voters do not exercise their right of inspection which they have regarding the behavior of politicians, and their attitude makes light of these candidates.

It is apparent that the game of representative democracy leads to the advantaging of profiteers, to the detriment of those who produce the wealth, to the advantage of those who seek to improve their condition by sponging on the incomes and savings of others. When a pressure group gains an advantage by pilfering from other people, it is not necessary to steal directly from those other persons. It is easier for the pressure group to get its money from the State. The modern State has thus become an immense machine for transferring funds from one group to another. As Bastiat said of the State: *"It is that giant fiction by means of which everybody strives to live at the expense of everyone else."*

Conclusion
The Future: What is to be Done?

There is no society of freedom and dignity, if each one of us, in his personal capacity, does not carry out his duties as a free man.
Jacques Garello[1]

Many readers - even if they are sympathetic to the ideas presented in this book, even if they recognize its implacable logic, - will still find liberalism completely utopian. In the French society whose background is absolute monarchy followed by Jacobinism, impregnated by more than a century of Marxism, used to the obsessive interventionism of successive governments, how can a liberal society see the light of day? Neither the parties of the right and still less those of the left, offer the least prospect in this respect. The short-lived political parties which in the past aspired to call themselves "liberal" have not thus far aroused any wild enthusiasm on the part of the electorate.

Evolution towards a liberal society can therefore be a goal only for the very long run, the first task of which is explaining what is at stake. That is why this book has been written. When we rest on clear ideas, we can spread liberal morality around ourselves, in particular in the family. We must teach our children to take command of their acts (responsibility), to respect others and the property of others, including the property of their brothers and sisters, and to acquire the on-going habit of exploring the world. This entails our giving them a freedom of action which grows at the same time as their sense of responsibility. We must also keep a sharp eye on what they get taught at school, and intervene unfailingly each time they are taught false things. Better still is forming links with other parents in this matter.

When one understands what liberalism is, one can call oneself a liberal with head held high. One can counter, without inhibition, all the idiocies voiced on the subject by corrupt governments and ignorant citizens.

Obviously one should vote for authentically liberal candidates when

---

1   A nos dirigeants. (To Our Leaders) Editions Albatros, 1985.

they present themselves. While we are waiting, however, for a liberal party to achieve some semblance of power, we must also defend freedom and responsibility at the heart of civil society, by supporting associations which exert direct and tireless pressure on government, central and local, for promoting these values in their respective spheres of action. In France these include: Contribuables Associés, SOS Education, Sauvegarde Retraites , La Fondation pour la recherché sur les Administsrations publiques.

In the U.S., there are many such institutions: The Heritage Foundation (www.heritage.org), CATO Institute (www.cato.org), and The Mises Institute (www.mises.org) are but three examples. Likewise, in the UK, the Adam Smith Institute (adamsmith.org) and the Institute of Economic Affairs (iea.org.uk) promote classical liberal or "libertarian" values.

We conclude with Professor Jacques Garello, President of The Association for Economic Freedom and Social Progress (L'Association pour la Liberté Economique et le Progrès Social, or ALEPS) and an indefatigable bearer of the liberal banner in France:

"Let's build freedom. Freedom will take care of the rest".[2]

---

2   *Programme pour un Président.* Editions Albatros. Paris. 1988.

APPENDIX A:

Bill of Rights (the First 10 Amendments) of the United States Constitution

Ratified by the necessary number of states effective December 15, 1791.

First Amendment – Establishment Clause, Free Exercise Clause; freedom of speech, of the press, and of assembly; right to petition:

Congress shall make no law respecting an establishment of religion, or prohibiting the free exercise thereof; or abridging the freedom of speech, or of the press; or the right of the people peaceably to assemble, and to petition the Government for a redress of grievances.

Second Amendment – Militia (United States), Sovereign state, Right to keep and bear arms:

A well regulated Militia being necessary to the security of a free State, the right of the people to keep and bear arms shall not be infringed.

Third Amendment – Protection from quartering of troops:

No Soldier shall, in time of peace be quartered in any house, without the consent of the Owner, nor in time of war, but in a manner to be prescribed by law.

Fourth Amendment – Protection from unreasonable search and seizure:

The right of the people to be secure in their persons, houses, papers, and effects, against unreasonable searches and seizures, shall not be violated, and no Warrants shall issue, but upon probable cause, supported by Oath or affirmation, and particularly describing the place to be searched, and the persons or things to be seized.

Fifth Amendment – due process, double jeopardy, self-incrimination, eminent domain:

No person shall be held to answer for a capital, or otherwise infamous crime, unless on a presentment or indictment of a Grand Jury, except in cases arising in the land or naval forces, or in the Militia, when in actual service in time of War or public danger; nor shall any person be subject for the same offence to be twice put in jeopardy of life or limb; nor shall be compelled in any criminal case to be a witness against himself, nor be deprived of life, liberty, or property, without due process of law; nor shall private property be taken for public use, without just compensation.

Sixth Amendment – Trial by jury and rights of the accused; Confrontation Clause, speedy trial, public trial, right to counsel:
In all criminal prosecutions, the accused shall enjoy the right to a speedy and public trial, by an impartial jury of the State and district wherein the crime shall have been committed, which district shall have been previously ascertained by law, and to be informed of the nature and cause of the accusation; to be confronted with the witnesses against him; to have compulsory process for obtaining witnesses in his favor, and to have the Assistance of Counsel for his defense.

Seventh Amendment – Civil trial by jury:
In suits at common law, where the value in controversy shall exceed twenty dollars, the right of trial by jury shall be preserved, and no fact tried by a jury, shall be otherwise re-examined in any court of the United States, than according to the rules of the common law.

Eighth Amendment – Prohibition of excessive bail and cruel and unusual punishment:
Excessive bail shall not be required, nor excessive fines imposed, nor cruel and unusual punishments inflicted.

Ninth Amendment – Protection of rights not specifically enumerated in the Constitution:
The enumeration in the Constitution, of certain rights, shall not be construed to deny or disparage others retained by the people.

Tenth Amendment – Powers of States and people:
The powers not delegated to the United States by the Constitution, nor prohibited by it to the States, are reserved to the States respectively, or to the people.

APPENDIX B:

Declaration of the Rights of Man and of the Citizen

Approved by the National Assembly of France, August 26, 1789

The representatives of the French people, organized as a National Assembly, believing that the ignorance, neglect, or contempt of the rights of man are the sole cause of public calamities and of the corruption of governments, have determined to set forth in a solemn declaration the natural, unalienable, and sacred rights of man, in order that this declaration, being constantly before all the members of the Social body, shall remind them continually of their rights and duties; in order that the acts of the legislative power, as well as those of the executive power, may be compared at any moment with the objects and purposes of all political institutions and may thus be more respected, and, lastly, in order that the grievances of the citizens, based hereafter upon simple and incontestable principles, shall tend to the maintenance of the constitution and redound to the happiness of all.

Therefore the National Assembly recognizes and proclaims, in the presence and under the auspices of the Supreme Being, the following rights of man and of the citizen:

Articles:
1. Men are born and remain free and equal in rights. Social distinctions may be founded only upon the general good.

2. The aim of all political association is the preservation of the natural and imprescriptible rights of man. These rights are liberty, property, security, and resistance to oppression.

3. The principle of all sovereignty resides essentially in the nation. No body nor individual may exercise any authority which does not proceed directly from the nation.

4. Liberty consists in the freedom to do everything which injures no one else; hence the exercise of the natural rights of each man has no limits except those which assure to the other members of the society the enjoyment of the same rights. These limits can only be determined by law.

5. Law can prohibit only such actions as are hurtful to society. Nothing may be prevented which is not forbidden by law, and no one may be forced to do anything not provided for by law.

6. Law is the expression of the general will. Every citizen has a right to participate personally, or through his representative, in its foundation. It must be the same for all, whether it protects or punishes. All citizens, being equal in the eyes of the law, are equally eligible to all dignities and to all public positions and occupations, according to their abilities, and without distinction except that of their virtues and talents.

7. No person shall be accused, arrested, or imprisoned except in the cases and according to the forms prescribed by law. Any one soliciting, transmitting, executing, or causing to be executed, any arbitrary order, shall be punished. But any citizen summoned or arrested in virtue of the law shall submit without delay, as resistance constitutes an offense.

8. The law shall provide for such punishments only as are strictly and obviously necessary, and no one shall suffer punishment except it be legally inflicted in virtue of a law passed and promulgated before the commission of the offense.

9. As all persons are held innocent until they shall have been declared guilty, if arrest shall be deemed indispensable, all harshness not essential to the securing of the prisoner's person shall be severely repressed by law.

10. No one shall be disquieted on account of his opinions, including his religious views, provided their manifestation does not disturb the public order established by law.

11. The free communication of ideas and opinions is one of the most precious of the rights of man. Every citizen may, accordingly, speak, write, and print with freedom, but shall be responsible for such abuses of this freedom as shall be defined by law.

12. The security of the rights of man and of the citizen requires public military forces. These forces are, therefore, established for the good of all and not for the personal advantage of those to whom they shall be entrusted.

13. A common contribution is essential for the maintenance of the public forces and for the cost of administration. This should be equitably distributed among all the citizens in proportion to their means.

14. All the citizens have a right to decide, either personally or by their representatives, as to the necessity of the public contribution; to grant this freely; to know to what uses it is put; and to fix the proportion, the mode of assessment and of collection and the duration of the taxes.

15. Society has the right to require of every public agent an account of his administration.

16. A society in which the observance of the law is not assured, nor the separation of powers defined, has no constitution at all.

17. Since property is an inviolable and sacred right, no one shall be deprived thereof except where public necessity, legally determined, shall clearly demand it, and then only on condition that the owner shall have been previously and equitably indemnified.

(Translation Prepared by Gerald Murphy (The Cleveland Free-Net). Distributed by the Cybercasting Services Division of the National Public Telecomputing Network (NPTN).)

APPENDIX C:

A Selection of Great Liberal Books

Treaties and Essays

Frédéric Bastiat. The Law
Selected Essays in Political Economy
Economic Sophisms

Etienne de la Boetie. The politics of Obedience : The Discourse of Voluntary Servitude.

Benjamin Constant. Principles of Politics Applicable to All Nations

Niall Ferguson. Empire: How Britain Made the Modern World

Milton Friedman. Free to Choose
Capitalism and Freedom

Friedrich von Hayek. The Road to Serfdom
The Constitution of Liberty

Paul Johnson. Modern Times: A History of the World from the 1920s to the 1990s

John Locke. Two Treaties of Government.

John Stuart Mill. On Liberty

Friedrich von Mises. Liberalism
Economic Policy

Johan Norberg. In Defense of Global Capitalism.

Thomas Paine. The Rights of Man.

Murray Rothbard. Man, Economy and the State.

Adam Smith. The Wealth of Nations

Alexis de Tocqueville. Democracy in America.

An Anthology

Pierre Manent. An Intellectual History of Liberalism.

Novels

Ayn Rand. Atlas Shrugged
             The Fountainhead
             We the Living

Most of these books are available through "Laissez Faire Books" , (www. lfb.org). A link to Amazon allows one to obtain the few that are not. In addition, many now in the public domain are downloadable as free PDF texts from the On Line Library of Liberty of the Liberty Fund (oll. libertyfund.org), and the Mises Institute (www.mises.org).

About the Author:

Jacques de Guerin was born in 1931 in Libourne, France. He is a French (classical) liberal economist and political activist. An engineer by training, he is an alumnus of the Ecole des Mines de Paris and holds a Master of Science from the University of Berkeley in California. From 1958 through 1993, he held positions with ExxonMobil and PSA Peugeot-Citroen, travelling or living in over 50 countries. He was a French alderman from 1977 to 1989, and mayor of Saint-Loubouer from 1995 to 2005. In 1993 and 1998 he was a Liberal (libertarian party) candidate for the French parliament.

A student of two Nobel Laureates in Economics, he frequently writes and lectures on the historic economist and humanist Frederic Bastiat. He is an active or founding member of several classical liberal and Austrian economics organizations including the Frédéric Bastiat Circle, ALEPS (the Association for Economic Freedom and Social Progress), Liberté Chérie, and the International Society for Individual Liberty. He is the Editor of The Collected Works of Frédéric Bastiat, ed. Jacques de Guenin (Indianapolis: Liberty Fund, 2011), and is a French Knight of the Order of Merit.

www.ingramcontent.com/pod-product-compliance
Lightning Source LLC
Chambersburg PA
CBHW052217270326
41931CB00011B/2389